BE A HATER:
A Polemic on the Hater Mindset

By

Wes Parham MBA Ph.D.

WEEW Publishing
Drwesparham.com
Dr.w.c.parham@gmail.com

Ordering Information:
Quantity sales. Special discounts are available on quantity purchases by corporations, associations, and others. For details, contact the publisher above.

Printed in the United States of America.

ISBN: 0999688405
ISBN-13: 978-0-9996884-0-3

DEDICATION

This book is dedicated to my family and loved ones. As well as all the thinkers, innovators, students, and friends who desire to think outside of the Hater Mindset. Let's be "haters" together.

CONTENTS

PART 1 –
INTRODUCTION

Chapter 1- My Journey to Hater Hood

"UNCLE WES YOU ARE JUST A HATER"
- Amor (my niece)

If it is not clear from the title of this book, let me begin by stating that I am unequivocally, vehemently, passionately, and unashamedly a HATER!!! And while I recognize that in today's society embracing this title is not only shocking but has the potential to cause an individual to be ostracized and isolated. My hope, is that by the end of this book that you will also declare yourself to be an unapologetic hater as well. However, I am not naïve. I do understand that in order for this to happen a few things must occur first. One of those things is that I must first clarify what I am defining as a hater. The term "hater" as it is commonly understood or conceptualized in contemporary society and vernacular is not one that is often sought after or admired. In fact as a culture and society we actually "hate haters". We not only hate haters we *love* to hate haters. We revel in the idea that we can shun or show disdain for people simply because they are haters. Consequently, I understand that if I am going to challenge individuals to brand themselves with this title, I will have to present *a very compelling* argument. Which I hope to do. I hope to present an argument that has implications for individuals, society, and culture as a whole. As an organizational scholar, my area of interest is the intersection between culture and individual thinking. Understanding what elements in organizational culture and culture as a whole, lead individuals to think, function, behave, and live better. And so my purpose for writing this book is to present a case designed to do just that. A case that will help the culture, organizations, and individuals to live, function, behave, and think better by offering a shifted paradigm with which to view dissent, relationships, and cognition. Better yet, I hope to present a case that will help you the reader to view dissent, relationships, and cognition through a different lens than most of contemporary culture. In order to do so I must define what meaning I am imbuing into the term hater and why I think it is a better alternative to what I am calling the "Hater Mindset".

However, before I begin to lay out my case I think it is important to note that while I gladly claim the title of hater now, I didn't always embrace the title with the vigor I currently do. In fact, at first, I didn't know that I was a hater at all. And had you asked me I, like so many others today, would have denied the accusation and adamantly denounced it as a term used to mischaracterize or slander my reputation. Like many of you reading, I existed in a world where a hater was the last thing that I wanted to be. To be "a hater" was to be shunned and/or isolated. It was to be relegated to a pariah in contemporary society, none of which are compelling reasons to want to be a hater. So naturally the question arises, what led to this dramatic shift in ideology? How did I transform from avoiding being labeled a hater by others to gladly labeling myself, and even proselytizing the message of being a hater?

While my journey to being a hater was riddled with situations, conversations, and experiences that helped push me in this direction, there were two distinct memories that I believe served as major catalysts on my voyage to haterhood. Neither memory was particularly important or meaningful in themselves, in fact, both were actually pretty funny. But they allowed me to make some observations that eventually helped me to identify and define what I call the "Hater Mindset". And they led me to embrace the concept of being a hater. Ironically, both these situations revolve around narratives that resulted in me being called a hater by others. And while I had been called a hater in previous contexts, the irony, humor, and resulting metacognition (thinking about my thinking) that was derived from these two situations stand out as key elements that launched me on my expedition from hater avoidance to the embrace and advocacy of haterhood.

Twilight:

The first of the two experiences to put me on the path of haterhood began with "Twilight". Not at twilight, but with Twilight. Twilight being the immensely popular movie and book series that emerged in the early 2000's and subsequently released several films from 2008-2012. And while millions of people flooded theaters to be direct witnesses of the love story that was Bella, Edward, and Jacob, my experience with the films can only be described as hearsay at worst and second hand at best. Although I never graced the theater to see any of the films, at the time the movies were being made both my career and community involvements required that I spend an immense amount of time with teenagers. And though I may have missed the Twilight train, the teenagers I worked with had not. In fact, I would argue that anyone who worked with teenagers at the time was sure to have been inundated with endless discussions of the twilight films, to the point that it was almost impossible to avoid having at least a cursory understanding of the series and its characters. And this is exactly where I found myself during this time period, being besieged with stories and debates about Edward, Bella, and Jacob.

My job at the time was working as a life skills teacher and life coach for one of the largest nonprofits in the state of Missouri. In this position, I was responsible for the development and subsequent instruction of a life skills curriculum for a cohort of 7th, 8th, and 9th graders, with whom I met with daily. My ultimate goal in this position was to help equip these students with skills and attributes that would help them succeed in the real world. The topics we covered ranged from leadership and responsibility to relationships and integrity. Simultaneously, outside of work, I was engaged with a local church in town to develop and teach curriculum to their youth group. I would meet with these students at least twice a week to cover many of the same topics that I would discuss with my cohort of students from work. Between these two different roles, my life consisted of constantly thinking about teenagers and their development, and trying to ensure that they had healthy perspectives in preparation for life. Enter Twilight.

Anyone who has ever worked with teenagers quickly learns that the informal conversations with teenagers are often more impactful than any formal instruction and dialogue. My mother, who had extensive experiences with teenagers herself through my siblings and I and our constant groups of friends at the house, phrased it this way "teenagers don't care about how much you know, until they know how much you care". Believing this statement and using it as the lens by which I engaged with my teens, it was only natural that I began to pay attention when discussions of "Team Edward" or "Team Jacob" began to waft through the air as I interacted with my students each day. It wasn't long before I would find myself sitting on the side of an impassioned debate about two boys, Edward and Jacob, competing for the love of a girl, Bella. My interest was piqued by watching how enthralled students were with these books and the films, especially the teenage young ladies. Eventually, after listening to several conversations I found that the allure of the story for the teenage ladies was the "loving relationship" between Edward and Bella.

Edward was the 21st century reimagining of a vampire. He didn't melt in the sunlight but instead his skin shined when illuminated by the rays of the sun, he didn't seek out humans to kill for their blood but instead used bags of blood that came from one place or another to feed his hunger. He wasn't menacing but was portrayed as reserved. In essence, he represented a stark departure from the archetype of a vampire in the 20th century. In addition to his departure from the historical vampire archetype, he was also imbued with all of the qualities that typically reside in the quintessential Romeo character of stories. He had a strong sense of justice and responsibility and was positioned as the good man warring against the darkness present in the world. Bella on the other hand, was portrayed as more of your normal molded teenager. She was not outgoing, but she was not shy. She was smart, but not a nerd. She wasn't the coolest girl at school, but she was also not the complete outcast. She occupied a space somewhere in between the cool kids and the outcast. The space where most teenagers believe themselves to be. This made her character easily accessible and relatable. While Jacob is also key to the Twilight story, he does not have a relevant part in my Twilight experience and thus I have left him out. However, if you would like to know more about him you can probably easily still Netflix the Twilight movies, or stop the nearest 20-30 year old and ask them, were they Team Jacob or Team Edward, and learn all you would like to know.

The intersection between the Twilight series and my hater journey occurred one day as I was listening to a group of my teenage female students discussing Edward and Bella. On this day, the young ladies shared with me that the draw of Edward and Bella's story was that Edward wanted to suck Bella's blood more than he has wanted to suck any humans blood before but because he "loves her", HE WON'T SUCK HER BLOOD. In this statement the ladies summarized the romance that had won so many teens over. A blood-sucking vampire wants to suck the blood of a teenage girl, but out of love he won't do it. This *paragon of affection and pinnacle example of love* was that the vampire would not eat her. The love that so many teenagers had found amazing and enthralling, this was it in a nutshell. I watched the faces of the teenagers I was talking with as they described the beauty of Edward and Bella's love, and described how they wanted a love like that. And while their faces were filled with joyous expression as they described this situation, I was facing a paradox of emotion. I wanted to laugh at the hilarity of the concept but at the same time, I was slightly saddened by the implications I believed were being drawn from this "love story". As I listened I recognized that these young ladies were essentially granting brownie points and attributing love to a man for NOT HURTING THE WOMAN HE LOVES. Not for his attentiveness to her needs, his ability to be able to recognize her unique beauty, his support for her as she changes and grows, or anything else. But instead, for NOT HURTING HER. That is essentially what it means for a vampire to want to eat someone but to choose not to. He is choosing to not hurt her.

I don't know if it was the burden I felt I carried to make sure that the teens I interact with were prepared for the world, and thus had healthy views of relationships. Or if it was the fact that I had recently been trying to help a couple of young ladies to think differently about abusive relationships they were in, but in either case I wanted to address this point with the teenage ladies I was talking with. And so I took the time to comically state my observation to them.

> *"You know you are saying this a good relationship because he wants to eat her but won't right?" I stated. "You don't get brownie points for not eating someone. That's like saying,*

14

'girl I know he loves me so much, because he wants to hit me but won't.' That's not love. You don't get brownie points for that. You girls have to demand more than that. If that's all you are asking for we are in bad shape!"

My statement while mixed with humor and sarcasm was meant to evoke some conversation, dialogue, or debate. I was hoping that the young ladies I was conversing with would at least ponder on the statements I said, or affirm to me that they do demand more in their relationships, or even combat my point with counterarguments. However, what I got instead I came to view as a far worse reaction. One of the young ladies simply turned to me and said "Mr. Wes, you a hater!" After which we all laughed, I made a few more jokes and they continued the conversation about Edward.

It wasn't until later as I had begun to see the use of the term hater in our society as a problem that I recognized what had happened in that moment. By simply stating that I was a hater, the ladies in the group had completely dismissed my point. And I don't mean dismissed in the critical thinking/debate sense. The dismissal that requires the allocating of emotional and cognitive weight to counter-evidence and discovering that counter-evidence is sufficient to refute whatever assertion is being made. But I mean dismissed as in never considered, evaluated, or compared. Dismissed as in no attempt at internalization or consideration. The point that I was making was never even discussed, acknowledged, countered, or validated. It never came back up in the conversation. It was essentially ignored. It was as if the idea never existed. At the time I didn't give it any thought because the situation was one where I was just joking around with some of my teenage students. The conversation didn't seem important. But as I began to be intentional about viewing the way that classifying a person as a hater is used in contemporary society, I began to recognize that this situation is actually indicative of a larger phenomenon in our society, and one that I don't think is taking us in the right direction. That phenomenon is the using of the hater classification as a way to ignore disagreement. This was the first observation and catalyst that launched me on my journey toward becoming a hater. And it was this observation, that set the stage for me to be so profoundly impacted by the second situation I plan to share on my voyage to haterhood. The story of my niece and the bike ride.

Bike Riding with My Niece:

If Edward, Jacob, and Bella were the igniting agents that spurred me into the shallow waters of reflection on the Hater Mindset, then it was the sentence "Uncle Wes You Are Just a Hater" spoken by my six-year-old niece that pushed me to explore the Mariana trench like depths of the topic. The shrill sound of my niece's voice reverberating in the air forming the syllables that would come together to make the sentence "You are Just a Hater" echoed in my mind at a frequency that could only be described as near unbearable. I sat dumbfounded in shock for 3-5 seconds pondering what had just happened. My shock was not due simply to the fact that this statement was made but its impact was exponentially magnified by two distinct elements that were present in the situation. The first was that this was coming from my niece, a child who I loved dearly and who I was sure reciprocated my adoration. One who to this day, if asked, "who loves you no matter what" she answers "you do Uncle Wes". How could this child attribute to me "hate" when it is clear that I love her so deeply? The second reason that these words stung so much was because I did

16

not know how in that moment I could ever be described as doing anything remotely connected to hate.

The scene was a warm spring afternoon. My family, consisting of my wife, our three children and I had gone over to help my mother with some things around her house. While there, my younger brother and sister, who like all of us in my family jump at the opportunity to be in each other's company, decided to join us along with their children. My brother is the doting father of one son and my sister is the proud mother of two children, a son and a daughter. It is this daughter, my niece, who had spoken the words that troubled me that afternoon. As we had finished the items my mother needed assistance with we all decided to venture outside to enjoy the weather and allow our children to play together. While outside some of the children began to ride their bicycles. My niece however was unable to participate in the bike riding festivities, as she had not yet learned to ride a bike. Nevertheless, she saw this as an excellent opportunity to rectify this situation. Knowing that her mother could confidently and brazenly be described as an "indoor person" she made her request to me. "Uncle Wes, could you teach me how to ride a bike?" In my opinion, there are some monumental moments in children's lives that leave an indelible mark on their memories. When they first learn to read, tasting their favorite food for the first time, or watching their very first episode of Teenage Mutant Ninja Turtles for example. To me learning to ride a bike is one of those monumental moments, and I was honored that my niece had selected me to be a part of this experience in her life. In her defense, I am sure she did not see this moment as monumental and did not identify me as her potential bike riding sage, because I was more qualified than her other uncle. In fact, I highly suspect it was because my children were the best bike riders of the bunch at the time, and she reasoned that her cousin's bike riding acumen must be attributed to their initial bike riding instruction, which was provided by me. In either case, I responded to her inquiry in the affirmative and began to instruct her in the complicated arts of bike riding. It was this decision that led to "the statement". After several minutes of instruction my niece was making some progress in generating momentum on the bicycle but little improvement in her capacity to determine which direction the momentum of the bike would or should go. In an effort to help her correct what was obviously a flaw in her steering procedure, I offered some additional instruction. "Hey baby, you can't jerk the wheel back and forth you have to focus on keeping it stable as you move forward". This was the moment that it happened. Although I am sure my mind is using hindsight bias to embellish the situation, as I think about what happened next I often visualize it as an almost cosmic event. The sky quickly darkened, the sound of large drums began to play ominously, and my niece looked at me with glaring eyes as the words she said exited her mouth in slow motion. UNCLE WES, YOU ARE JUST A HATER". In actuality, the situation must have been much less dramatic as my reply to her was something simple like "no baby nothing about what I'm doing is hateful." However, in light of the role her words played in leading me to this point, I am inclined to hold onto my revised version of the memory.

The exchange between my niece and I that day should not have been a life changing moment, and if it weren't for its role in launching me on my journey to "being a hater" it would probably be easily forgotten. Faded from my mind and replaced with more recent and vivid memories. Whether it was because Edward and Bella had already caused me to begin to cogitate on the concept of a hater, or because the irony of the situation was so pronounced (I mean I could not imagine a more loving situation than an uncle stepping into the role usually reserved for parents, to teach his niece to ride a bike), I began to think constantly about what happened. The event that I thought would leave an indelible mark on the memory of my niece, had the reverse effect and became imprinted deeply in my own psyche. I became not just fascinated by what my niece said, but the way she said it. "You are just a hater". It was such a common phrase, but one that seemed infused with so much meaning. Before that day those five words would have passed by me without a second thought, but post the statement I began to hear them everywhere, each time poking and prodding at my conscience. Bombarding me with questions. What did these individuals mean when they said this sentence? What did it say about them and their thinking? What did it mean for the person being labeled a hater? What did it say about their relationship to the person labeling them a hater? What underlying ideas, viewpoints, worldviews, and assumptions motivate the thinking behind calling someone a hater? In a very real sense my niece had started me on a journey that I couldn't escape and that would eventually lead me to the ideas that I espouse in this book.

Hater and Hater Mindset

Astute readers will recognize at this point that although I have laid the groundwork for much of what I plan to discuss in this book, I have not yet defined the two terms that I used at the beginning of this chapter, Hater and Hater Mindset. It is to this purpose that I now turn. However, simply defining the terms Hater and the Hater Mindset is not enough. In order to truly persuade you to join me on the journey to being a hater, I must also simultaneously explain why my conception of the term hater rivals or should supersede the current definition that is associated with the idea of a hater. And to do this I must not only offer the merits of my position, but I must also expose the errors that I feel exist in the contemporary conceptions of a hater. And as a final piece I must synthesize all of this information in such a way that you the reader find my argument convincing enough to embrace my ideology. It is this understanding that frames the remaining structure of this book. My goal in writing this book is to layout a convincing argument for choosing to be a hater as an alternative to the cognitive philosophy I define as the Hater Mindset And my hope is that you will be sufficiently persuaded by my arguments and join me in actively countering the Hater Mindset in culture and embracing my definition and worldview of a hater moving forward.

So what is the difference between the two terms, Hater and Hater Mindset? Semantically they seem the same, and a reader simply seeing the terms without added context would easily assume that the terms are interchangeable. To answer the question of distinction, I think a simple examination of the contemporary use of the word hater could be useful. In contemporary culture when someone calls someone else a hater, they usually have one particular meaning in mind. "You (the person being called a hater, the labeled) are offering and holding a perspective that is different than the one that I (the person calling someone a hater, the labeler) am currently holding, and thus you are a hater". This is essentially what being a hater is in contemporary culture. To disagree with someone. More accurately for someone to disagree with "me". Those who utilize hater in this way often try to shroud this fact behind philosophies and rhetoric of haters being people who don't want to see you succeed. Or people who just want to pull you down. If you ask them to define what a hater is, you may hear them say a hater is someone who wants to stop you from reaching your potential. But, the usage of the term in most people's vocabulary reveals that this is not actually who they believe a hater to be. Think back to the instances when you have either called someone a hater, been called a hater, or heard someone else called a hater. The reason that the individual was labeled a hater was most likely because they were asserting a perspective that the other individual in the conversation did not agree with. In most cases, the "hater" or person labeled as such, was not targeting the labeler, but simply offering a different perspective which the labeling individual did not like. There was no attempt to sabotage or pull down the labeling individual, only an expression of disagreement or alternative perspective. It is as simple as that. In today's culture a hater is someone with a perspective that conflicts with your own. And that alternative perspective causes them to be labeled a "hater". This is the idea that the teenage young lady and my niece had in mind when they called me a hater. They did not think I was jealous of them or wanted to hold them back. Instead, I was holding a view that they currently disagreed with. Thus in current culture a formal definition of a hater could be defined as:

> **A person who holds a position, opinion, view, or perspective that is different from the position, opinion, view, or perspective that you currently hold.**

We will call this the flawed hater concept or the contemporary understanding of a hater. It is this definition of a hater that I believe leads to the Hater Mindset. The conception of a hater as someone who has a different position than the one you currently hold, while simplistic in definition, I believe is actually quite problematic. It is problematic because linked to this conception are three underlying cognitive implications. Implications that I argue throughout this book are problematic for culture

21

and society. The first implication is that this conception of a hater indicates that the labeling individual (the person calling someone a hater) does not like and/or is not willing to consider dissent, disagreement, or alternative perspectives. In fact, the idea that an individual holding a different perspective is attributed with "hate" or called a "hater" (not a disliker, a dissenter, or even a negative ninny) seems to suggest that this dismissal and disdain for dissent and disagreement by the labeler is intensely held. So intensely held that it attributes one of the strongest words for dislike in the English language, "hate", to the differing individual. The second implication I believe comes from this conception of "hater" is that it makes no attempt to justify, defend, or explain the views, actions, or whatever element is occurring, that the labeling individual is doing. It actually just assumes that it is ok for this person to have their belief, action, behavior, etc. simply because they want to. It says that the labeling individual is *entitled* to whatever view they are holding. The third implication is that it causes the labeling individual to devalue the person they are calling a hater. The label of "a hater" allows the labeling individual to diminish the importance and value that they attribute to the labeled individual. They are justified in not caring as much about the person because they are of course "just a hater".

I believe that these three implications result in cognitive behaviors and assumptions that I dub throughout this book as "the Hater Mindset". I formally define the Hater Mindset as:

> **the mindset that labels others a hater due to their dissenting views and predisposes individuals to lower levels of critical thinking, innovation, tolerance of dissent, and epistemic**

motivation. While also fostering a mindset of entitlement, and a devaluing of relationships.

This book is about identifying this mindset in culture, and elevating it to a level of conscious visibility. Much of my argument is based on the idea that the Hater Mindset functions below the surface at an implicit and subconscious level. This book is about exposing these hidden workings, making them visible so that they can be countered. I hope to challenge us as a culture to not support the current conception of a hater and its accompanying Hater Mindset. Instead, I hope to redefine and rebrand the term "hater" as a counter to the Hater Mindset. Challenging us as a culture to "Be A Hater". This approach I believe will make us better thinkers, more empathetic, less polarized, and more appreciative of dissent and diversity. Basically, we will think, function, behave, and live better.

The concept of a "hater" as I hope to re-conceptualize it in this book then, is scaffolded on top of the Hater Mindset. That is, that by understanding one, you can glean the meaning of the other. In this case being a hater as I have conceptualized it can be formally defined as:

A person who actively combats the Hater Mindset, by pursuing dissent, doubting their own cognitive entitlement and applying value to existing relationships and new relationships even in the midst of disagreement.

This definition I have titled the "hater revised" definition. For me, being a hater is to act opposite of the underlying assumptions and implications associated with the contemporary understanding of the word hater. In other words to counter the Hater Mindset. I am using the terms flawed hater concept, hater revised definition and Hater Mindset as cognitive frameworks that can essentially govern the way that an individual interacts with the world on multiple levels. They can in effect define how you will view, and how you will react to the words "You Are Just A Hater".

Framework of this book

As I began to write this book I thought it was only fitting that since the sentence "You are just a hater" played such an important role in initiating my examination of the Hater Mindset, that it serve as a focal point for the discussions shared in this text. As an avid reader, many of my favorite books are those that provide strong and well thought out ideas in tandem with an easy to remember structure for those arguments. There have been so many books where I was amazed as the writers offered breathtaking assertions supported wonderfully with examples and research and written in masterful prose, only for me to complete the book and be overwhelmed with all of the arguments presented and struggling to create an overarching structure in which the ideas could be placed to help me retain them in my memory. And while I will leave the determination of whether my arguments and assertions are worthy of being described as breathtaking to you, I do believe that the overarching structure by which I present them is one that can be easily recalled to memory. That is because each of the arguments are centered on one of the words spoken to me by my niece that day, "You are just a Hater". Embedded in these words are the philosophical underpinnings, underlying assumptions, and adamantly held cognitive beliefs I plan to address and refute. The chapters in this book are divided into sections that focus on the embedded meanings present in the words "You are just a hater". The construction of my ideas then are based on the deconstruction and examination of the elements present in these words. Thus, each section begins by identifying which word in the sentence is being addressed allowing for all the arguments of the text to be concomitant with one of the words in the "you are just a hater" sentence. Hopefully allowing for an easy way to structure this book and easily remember its arguments. The last section of the book diverges from this structure and outlines my redefinition of the word "hater" and why I think it should be embraced. However, before I dive into my thoughts on the "You are just a hater" declaration, I think it is only fitting that I explain why I think that a book like this is needed. For me a polemic on the Hater Mindset is needed because of the mindsets pervasiveness. And what better way to discuss the pervasiveness of the Hater Mindset than with Taylor Swift.

Chapter 2 – Taylor Swift: The Most Dangerous Person in the World

"Hater"
– Everybody, Everywhere

In 2014 while working for a college in the Midwest, I began to make a statement that most people, myself included, would view as completely outrageous. And in many cases making the statement led me into some very interesting conversations. I would regularly state that Taylor Swift was the most dangerous person in the world. I made the statement so often that it began to be something I was known for in certain circles. Impassioned "swifties" (Taylor Swift fans), curious observers, and amusement seekers alike, for different reasons and on numerous occasions sought to draw out my thoughts on Taylor Swift. Individuals would say to their friends, "hey ask him about Taylor Swift and see what he says", hoping to draw me into a diatribe of the dangers of the "Shake it Off" singer. On one occasion, one individual handed me a flyer to let me know that Taylor Swift was in town on that very day to see what reaction might be provoked in me through this revelation. I told them that I was going to the concert, but only to picket Taylor during the event (I didn't really go).

To be fair, while I made this statement often, it was not a statement I meant in earnest. It was actually used as a way to break the ice with college students who were on my campus for a high stakes interview. The students would arrive on campus prepared to interview for a position in a highly selective healthcare education program. The program usually received somewhere between 900-1000 applications and had around a 10%

acceptance rate. Needless to say, the students who were selected for an interview were arriving on campus with high levels of anxiety, nervousness, and stress. My role at the time was to facilitate their interview process. And for me, part of this role included helping the students to feel more at ease and lower their anxiety levels before their interviews. In an effort to do this, as the students arrived in the morning, I would make jokes about school, other students, my family, music, etc. The reference to Taylor Swift as the most dangerous person in the world was birthed out of this context. A way to lighten the mood at the beginning of the students' day. And while this is how the statement started, I found the saying, "there is always some truth in jest" to be true in this case. As my examination of the Hater Mindset progressed, I began to believe there were several gems of truth that could be unearthed through digging deeper into my joke/argument that Taylor Swift is the most dangerous person alive. Gems that would illustrate more about the pervasive nature of the Hater Mindset.

Pervasiveness being the purpose for the next two chapters, and arguably this book. The need for a polemic on the Hater Mindset does not exist if the mindset itself is not pervasive in the culture. If there are only a handful of individuals who possess the Hater Mindset and its associated behaviors, they could easily be ignored or discredited and thus there would be no need to engage them in debate whether written or any other form. It is the pervasiveness of ideas that call out into the abyss of culture, requiring the resonant sound of a response back. I have yet to check, but I am quite confident that there are no refutations or polemics written on the topic of belief in unicorns. Nor do I see individuals engaging in public debate of any kind about squirrels beaming mind control waves into the brains of humans (though with some of the craziness on Facebook this would explain a lot). The

28

reason neither of these topics have necessitated publicly vigorous opponents, besides the fact that to engage them in debate is to look as off-kilter as the arguments themselves, is that they are not pervasive enough to require it. The existence of an idea, however erroneous, may not always require a public refutation. But ideas that are pervasive, especially dangerous ones, are ones that must be addressed. The ideas that have crept into the culture, embedding themselves in its fabric, and directing the worldview of its members, these ideas should be addressed, and addressed publicly. This leads to a logical query for this book. Is the Hater Mindset truly pervasive in today's culture? If it is not pervasive, then to this point I have wasted your time and mine discussing the ideas of a small subset of individuals that may have no important effect on your life moving forward. My hope, however, is to show that this is not the case. To show that the Hater Mindset is not just erroneous but everywhere. This is where the propositions that formed my argument about Taylor Swift can be helpful. The propositions offer a glimpse of the evidence and rationale for why I believe the Hater Mindset has been and continues to be pervasive in contemporary culture.

The Hater Mindset Swift-ly Crossing the Culture!!

My joke about Taylor Swift being the most dangerous person in the world was developed after the release of her 2014 hit song "Shake it Off". While I haven't the time, space, or energy to transcribe all the lyrics from the song, which may all be relevant to our discussion, the hook from the song provides an overall context for the song's general theme. The hook lyrics state

" Cuz a haters gonna hate, hate, hate, hate, hate and a player's gonna play, play, play, play, play.

Baby I'm just gonna shake, shake, shake, shake, shake. Shake it Off. Shake it Off" [1]

For me this song could serve as the symbolic Bill of Rights, Declaration of Independence, or even Articles of Faith for the Hater Mindset. Outlining the three specific beliefs and values of those who would embrace and champion this mindset. A devaluing of individuals, a disdain and dismissal of dissent, and an entitlement to personal ideas and beliefs.

The chorus starts by stating, "haters are going to hate". This lyric while short implies several things. It implies that "haters" are not individuals who warrant attention or consideration. They are not individuals that you need to value. Whatever assertion they are making is just hating, and they are just hating because that is what they do. You need not value them or their opinions.

If you combine the devaluing of haters with the idea that, a **hater is someone who holds a different view from the one you currently hold,** discussed in the last chapter, you find a larger argument forming. This combination actually advocates for the dismissal and disdain of dissent. According to the lyrics, people who disagree with you (haters) are just hating because that is what they do. Their points are not valid and don't need to be considered because they are simply haters hating. So why listen to them or engage with their opinions? Instead, their dissent should be dismissed or disdained.

The lyric following the "haters gonna hate" lyric in the chorus is the lyric "player's gonna play". The positioning of the "players gonna play" lyric directly after the "haters gonna hate" lyric juxtaposes a player as the opposite of a hater. Players are in essence any individual who is not a hater. Which is of course you…, and me…, and really most people in contemporary culture who would view the term hater negatively. We are the players, because we are certainly not the haters, right? And since we are players we "gonna play". That is, those who would classify themselves as players (which is most people) should just do whatever it is they want to do. "Players gonna play" of course. Players in this view don't have to account for or explain themselves, their beliefs, or their actions. Instead, they are entitled to them. They are players and they "gonna play". It's what they are expected to do.

When hearing the "Shake it Off" song I was struck by how overt and blatant the song proclaimed the Hater Mindset. Most of my other interactions with the Hater Mindset were through subtle almost covert messages that were underlying less abrasive and controversial experiences. While "Shake it Off" made no such attempts. It flagrantly stated that it did not like or consider dissent, that it devalued haters, and that it celebrated individuals not having to explain their behavior, thinking, or actions.

After my exposure to "Shake it Off" I burrowed into many of Swift's other songs and discovered remnants of the "Shake it Off" themes in several of her other songs as well. In "Bad Blood" the devaluing of a relationship is the central theme. The songs "Blank Space" or "Call it What You Want" focus on cognitive entitlement and not having to explain your actions, as well as disdaining dissent about your decisions. Swift's 2017 album *Reputation* is full of these concepts including her song "I Did Something Wrong", where she says

> "They said I did something wrong. Then why's it feel so good?...And I'd do it over and over again ..."

Before I knew it, I had become an avid listener to the musical compositions of Taylor Swift and found the themes of the Hater Mindset ran through much of her music (some of you probably think at this point this is all a ruse so I can listen to Taylor's music). These recurring themes led me to make the joke/assertion that Taylor Swift was the most dangerous person in the world because she was instrumental in propagating the Hater Mindset on a massive level. And while my thoughts in this chapter focus on Swift, it is important to note that she is not alone in her promulgation of the Hater Mindset. In fact, the ideas of dismissing and disdaining dissent, devaluing dissenting relationships, and cognitive entitlement are ideas that have been in music for decades. They can be found in songs as early as "My Prerogative" by Bobby Brown, which came out in 1988, to songs like "Pop Ya Collar" by Usher that came out in 2001. Swift's contemporary and "frenemy", Kanye West, released a free mixtape titled "Can't Tell Me Nothing" in 2007. Which in its very title advocates for the dismissal of dissent. You literally can't tell him nothing. And VH1 even put out a list in 2014 of the top "shake off the haters" songs. A quick internet search of the terms "hater" and "lyrics" produces over 9 million results. One result from this search generates a list of songs that are written about haters and is over 231 pages long itself. These search results make it pretty apparent that the promotion of the Hater Mindset is not restricted to Taylor Swift. But can be found in the music of several artist throughout all different types of musical genres.

It is important to note however, that it's not just music promoting the Hater Mindset either. I have found the Hater Mindset themes promoted in TV shows (the 2016-2017 show "Haters Back Off!), internet posts (the get the haters off the internet Facebook post), movies (the whole Bad Santa, Bad Mom, etc. genre of movies) and almost every crevice of contemporary society. Thus, while this chapter focuses on Taylor Swift my points are not meant to be confined to Taylor Swift, but instead are to be used as a working example of how the Hater Mindset has become so pervasive in the culture.

My argument for Taylor Swift's potential peril to the world was built on four propositions.

1) Millennials (and by extension generation Z) are the largest generation in American History[2]
2) Millennials (and generation z) listen to on average 75% more music (and other media) than previous generations. Thus, they have high levels of exposure to the language, vernacular, worldviews, and beliefs transmitted through that media.
3) The language and words people use and hear influence their attitudes, beliefs, and assumptions. And this occurs even if this language is through music (or other media).
4) The themes of Taylor Swift's message (the Hater Mindset) are implicitly and subconsciously accepted by individuals through their exposure to music (and media).

Taken together, these propositions address three key questions related to the pervasiveness of the Hater Mindset. Why does it matter if the Hater Mindset is pervasive in the culture? This question is addressed by proposition 1. Is the Hater Mindset actually pervasive in the culture? This question is addressed by propositions 2 and 3. And how did this mindset become pervasive in the culture? Which is addressed by proposition 4. The rest of this chapter as well as chapter 3 use the four propositions above to answer these three questions. My hope is that by examining these three questions and their related propositions it will shed light on the issue of the pervasiveness of the Hater Mindset in today's culture.

Why does it Matter?

Proposition 1 of the Taylor swift argument addresses the "why" question related to the pervasiveness of the Hater Mindset. Why does it matter if the Hater Mindset is pervasive? The proposition states that Millennials, which have been described as the individuals born between 1982-1999[3] or 1980-2000[4] (in either case I'm in this range) are the largest generation in American history. And while this is true, I don't believe it tells the whole story in terms of the culture of Millennials. I would argue that to limit the unique attributes of the Millennial generation to America is like trying to examine the Empire State Building by inspecting a single brick. Or condensing all of astrophysics down to the statement that the universe is expanding. Or making judgements on Harry Potter after only seeing one movie and reading none of the books (which I did and have been told a thousand times that this was a mistake). What I mean is that globalization and technology have effectively shrunk the world, and by doing so diminished many of the differences in thinking and values that use to exist due to geography. I once saw individuals from several different countries debating on the internet about who won the Nas vs Jay-Z rap battle. Clearly the answer is Nas, I would take his Ether track over SuperUgly by Jay-Z any day, but that is not my point. The reason this situation is interesting is that these individuals were familiar with both Nas and Jay-Z and they were able to engage in a debate regarding style, references, and harshness that just a generation ago might have seemed foreign to individuals from such geographically spread out countries. But now, due to globalization and technology, they can share a similar culture despite their geographic differences. So while for simplicity, and the purposes of this discussion we will focus on the Millennial generation in terms of America, we do this recognizing that many of these themes could be applied to a larger global context.

The simple answer to the question "why does it matter if the Hater Mindset is pervasive" was clearly and concisely stated by Thom and Jess Rainer in their text, *The Millennials: Connecting to America's Largest Generation*[5]. They write, "if we don't learn more about this generation (millennials), we are doing them and ourselves a disservice. They are just too big to ignore". As the largest generation in American History with over seventy-eight million live births[6] (and generation Z close behind with 72 million[7]), Millennials *are* too big to ignore. In their book MILLENNIALS: *A Portrait of Generation Next* Paul Taylor and Scott Keeter[8] argue that generations like people have personalities. Beliefs, ideas, worldviews, and perspectives that can be characterized as generally accepted and valued by that generation. And Millennials are no different. These values, attitudes, beliefs, and behaviors permeate each aspect of the Millennial's life, from the workplace[9], to interpersonal relationships[10], and even intrapersonal reflection[11]. As such, an understanding of these values, attitudes, beliefs, and behaviors are of paramount importance for the world. "Millennials are already impacting businesses, the workplace, schools, churches, and many more organizations"[12]. As a generation, they are poised to cause a massive shift in contemporary culture. I propose that this shift includes the Hater Mindset as an accepted part of the values or personality of the culture.

For me, the fear with this shift, is that it is occurring on a *cultural* level. The emphasis on culture here is intentional. The term culture in today's vernacular functions as a catch all for every element of human existence. You can hear people explain almost every aspect of human behavior as a direct function of their "culture". Culture explains the soap people use, their ethnic background, their hobbies; I have heard people attribute a choice of Cheetos (flaming hot vs extra flaming hot) to culture. So it could appear almost meaningless when I use the word culture throughout this book. But, as an organizational scholar the term "culture" has a very distinct meaning. Edward Schein (2010) a prominent organizational scholar wrote that culture is:

> a pattern of shared basic assumptions that the group learned as it solved its problems of external adaptation and internal integration that has worked well enough to be considered valid and, therefore, to be taught to new members as the correct way to perceive, think, and feel in relation to those problems.[13]

The key elements in Schein's definition are that culture provides individuals with the "correct way to perceive, think, and feel" and this information is therefore supposed to "be taught to new members". In essence, culture is a set of cognitive beliefs and behaviors that are meant to be passed on. This is essentially, what people mean today when they say culture. They are attempting to explain why a person behaves a certain way, and attributing that behavior to something that was passed down to them.

However, in most cases where people refer to culture, the goal is not to alter said behavior, but just to observe why it occurred. Attributing an individual's actions to their culture is often used as a justification for *not* trying to change this behavior. Hence, I was told you don't try to switch someone from flaming hot to extra flaming hot Cheetos, because that is their culture. This is because culture is not easily changed. Once an element has been embedded into a culture it can become very difficult to uproot it. Edward Schein says this is because these behaviors are often passed down and accepted subconsciously. Which is exactly what I am proposing is occurring in terms of the Hater Mindset in contemporary culture (this will be discussed more in the next chapter). I am proposing that the danger in the Hater Mindset is that it is being embedded in the culture of the largest generation in American History. This makes it dangerously pervasive, as it will not be something that can be easily uprooted. If the Hater Mindset is woven into the fabric of the culture of the largest generation in history than it is also on course to have a potentially huge impact on the world and generations to come. For me this is the answer to the question "why it matters if the Hater Mindset is pervasive." In short because Millennials are just too big to ignore.

Is the Hater Mindset Really Pervasive?

If proposition 1 of the Taylor Swift argument addresses the "why" question of the pervasiveness of the Hater Mindset, than propositions 2 and 3 address the "is" question. Is the Hater Mindset really pervasive? The two interrelated propositions that address this question focus on the unique relationship between music (and other popular media by extension) and culture, as proof that the Hater Mindset is pervasive in the culture.

As I shared earlier, my examination of Taylor Swift began with her 2014 song "Shake it Off". A YouTube count of the song in April of 2017 reports that the YouTube video itself had been viewed 2,048,535,462 times. Yep, you read that correctly 2,048,535,462. That is over 2 billion times on YouTube alone. This does not account for streaming plays, downloads, album sales, etc. The U.N. estimates that there are around 7 billion people in the world[14]. If you were to subtract a couple million views to account for me listening to the song (we'll say for research purposes not because the song is super catchy) that is still enough views for almost a third of the human race to have seen or heard the song at least once. This means that the "Shake it Off" song by all standards would be classified as indisputably popular, and the popular music of a society plays a uniquely dichotomous role in both the reflecting and shaping of the culture of that society.

Ethnomusicologist for years have observed this dichotomous relationship. They argue that music serves as a reflection of culture *and* helps to shape what the culture looks like. In terms of reflection, ethnomusicologist Alan Merriam made this point in the early 1960's. He wrote that one of the functions of music is "symbolic representation"[15]. This is the idea that music uses words and symbols that convey values, beliefs, and ideals. Most often these are the values, beliefs, and ideals that are widely held in the culture. Musicians chronicle the beliefs and ideals of a culture through song, and those songs become sounding boards echoing the ideas and values of the culture back to the culture's members. One writer states that this echo of ideas back to the culture is actually what explains why people like the music that they do[16]. People like the popular music of a culture because they feel their popular music represents them, their values, and their beliefs. Thus, the music of a given generation, society, or culture can serve as a sort of manifesto for what that group values and believes. It exhibits the ideas, values, and beliefs that are pervasive in the culture. This is why songs like Marvin Gaye's "What's Going On", or Bob Dylan's "These times are a changing" or in the case of Millennials DJ Khaled's "All I do is Win" (or maybe that one is just mine) are often referred to as theme songs for movements. They reflect the prominent ideals and values present in the culture at that time. This is also why you and I probably have a song (or a few songs) that serve as soundtracks for periods of our lives. When we hear them, they remind us of what we believed and felt at the time. For me it is the Sesame Street song. That Big Bird really had his finger on the pulse of my life. As Merriam said, our popular music provides us with "symbolic representation". And echoes our thoughts back to us.

In the case of Millennials, technology has taken this echoing of ideas to the next level. The creation of iPods, mp3 players, streaming music, etc. has increased access to music significantly. This increase in access has been accompanied by an increase in usage. Millennials have a well-documented affinity for music. A recent example that emphasizes the value of music to Millennials is the popular rapper and producer, Dr. Dre. In 2014, Dr. Dre just missed becoming a billionaire (with a B) after selling his stake in his "Beats Headphones" company[17]. The value of his headphones company designed to create a stylistic and vibrant listening experience was estimated to be worth billions of dollars with the bulk of that value being attributed to Millennials. And Millennial's value of music is not just anecdotal either. A Pew Research study in 2011 found that 74% of Millennials owned and used a portable music device of some sort on a daily basis[18]. This usage is estimated at 3-6 hours of music a day[19]. That is a lot of exposure to music. And surveys on Generation Z report that Generation Z members have about the same exposure, with them utilizing a portable music device approximately 3 hours a day[20].

If ethnomusicologists are right and the popular music of a culture reflects the ideals, values, and beliefs of that culture, and people listen to popular songs because they represent the values, ideals and beliefs of their life; than what does a song that has been listened to over 2 billion times on just one single outlet say. It clearly must say something about the values of that culture. I think it implies that there is something in the song that connects with the values and beliefs of individual listeners and the larger culture. Something that they value and view as reflective of their own cultural values. I would propose that the song serves as a sort of mirror reflecting and confirming back to the culture the values that the culture currently holds. And that reflection is of the Hater Mindset. And with over 2 billion YouTube views, it can most certainly be described as pervasive.

However, the 2 billion views of "Shake it Off" also play another important role in explaining the pervasiveness of the Hater Mindset in contemporary culture. This role is identified in proposition three of the Taylor Swift argument. The proposition that

- The language and words people hear and use influence their attitudes, beliefs, and assumptions.

This proposition implies that not only does Swift's "Shake it Off" reflect the Hater Mindset as a value that is present in the culture, but it also helps to shape the culture with the Hater Mindset as a part of it. This is what I meant when I described music as having a dichotomous role in relationship to culture. Music not only reflects culture, it shapes it.

The idea of songs being used to shape culture is not new. In fact, the practice of writing songs to affect culture is so prevalent that a title for these types of songs was developed, "protest music". James Brown's "Say it Loud I'm Black and I'm Proud" which was written to challenge African-Americans to change the way they thought about being black, and Bob Marley's "I Shot the Sheriff" which was written as a way to challenge police oppression are examples of protest songs. Both songs were written with the goal of not only reflecting the culture but also helping to shape it. And quite often, music is successful in helping to shape culture. To see how this occurs we turn to the field of linguistics.

Talk How I Talk, Think Like I Think

Linguist have long known, that the words a person uses, also known as there idiolect shapes their perception of reality and the world. In fact, the idea that the language a person uses shapes how they view the world has been thoroughly explored by research in multiple science fields over the past century. Lera Boroditsky, an Assistant Professor of cognitive psychology at Stanford University, writes, "studies have shown that changing how people talk changes how they think"[21]. The political scholar Ostrom wrote:

> "The words we use and the relationships we assume by virtue of the words we use determine the thoughts we have, the implications we draw, and the conclusions we reach"[22].

In the book *Whole Person Care: A New Paradigm for the 21st century,* Dr. Abraham Fuks, a medical doctor, writes, "the words we use form the mental models of our lived worlds and shape our perceptions, understandings, and meanings"[23]. In essence, the words we use determine how the mind will look at the world.

Take for example the word "Nazi". Because of the historical significance of this word, you have probably created a mental model for a Nazi. This mental model frames how you view individuals who would, for instance, call themselves "Neo-Nazi's" even if you don't know what they believe. This is because the mental model you created by your word use affects how you see people, groups, beliefs, environments, and the world. Our brains

41

use mental models to determine right and wrong, friend or foe, love or hate and more. And these models are framed by language. Thus our language shapes our worldview, our ideals, our values, and our beliefs.

I can imagine at this point a contrarian reader (most likely an *avid* Taylor Swift fan) saying that while the assertion that an individual's word use influences their worldview is interesting, it does not address the propositions I offered. It doesn't explain how hearing the song "Shake it Off" could be, *or is being*, used to shape culture. It at most explains how it could shape Taylor Swift's view of the world. Since she is the one using the words, it would make sense that the song shapes her worldview, based on this rationale. To this I say, "touché critically thinking reader, you're right" (I hope that was you, I was impersonating)! Understanding that *our* own language shapes *our* worldview is only half of the proposition. It doesn't explain how the language we hear in songs and other media can shape our worldview or the worldview of the larger culture. That is unless, there is some sort of reciprocal relationship between our language and the language we hear used around us. If somehow the two were able to influence and shape each other.

Interestingly enough, this an observation that Clay Beckner from the University of New Mexico and his team made in a recent paper[24]. Beckner and his team point out that idiolects and communal language, the former being individual language and the latter being the language of the shared culture, are interdependent entities. Meaning that the language an individual uses and the language a culture uses are linked together. They influence and shape each other. As an example, I have recently been amazed at how much people have begun to use the "slay" after Beyoncé' (one of the most popular artists in the world, in case you've been asleep for the last 14 years or so) said the word "slay" in her song

42

"formation". You would think that "slay" was taught as basic grammar in elementary schools, the way it is used so often in social media posts, conversations, text messages, and other outlets. It has become a common term in the language of contemporary culture and of individuals within the culture. And people have not only adopted the usage of the word slay but they have embraced the meaning Beyoncé has imbued into the term as well. Beyoncé's usage of the term slay in her music impacted both the usage and meaning of the word slay in the vocabulary of the culture and individuals within the culture. This is a template type example of the interdependent relationship of individual language and cultural language. It shows how the language individuals hear used around them shapes their own language and by extension their worldview. The exposure to the language used by Beyoncé in her song formation influenced individual's usage of the term "slay" and even added new meaning to the term. This usage and meaning was adopted by several users in the culture until it became the language of the culture itself. Thus illustrating how individual language and communal language are interdependent.

We all recognize this interdependent relationship intuitively. Think about the language you use every day. It is probably similar to the language that your friends use. The language you use, your friends use. And the language your friends use, you use, until it becomes the shared language of your group. Your language usage influences your friends' usage and your friends language usage influences your language usage. We have all heard the person with the over usage of the word "dude" or the person who still uses "da Bomb". I myself have been told that I say the phrase "does that make sense" far too often. Which is essentially my scholarly way of saying "nahwhatamsayin" (that is "you know what I am saying", for those who couldn't decode the phrase. When we hear these phrases we expect that the people using them have a social group or culture that also uses these phrases. This is because we know that individual language usage and communal language usage have a reciprocal interdependent relationship where they shape each other.

The reason that this reciprocal relationship is so easily observed between individuals and their friend groups is that our friends represent a major component of our social contexts. As Beckner and company write in the second point relevant to our discussion, the "rise and fall of linguistic forms" an individual uses is shaped primarily by their social contexts[25]. What the authors mean is that the language an individual hears and experiences around them in their social context determines what words and language they use more or less often. The language of our social contexts is what shapes our own language and by extension our opinions, values, and worldview. This makes music and other media exceptionally powerful in shaping our language.

Music and media, like friends, are fundamental parts of a culture's and an individual's social contexts. They are used for entertainment, relaxation, and other social activities. And this is no different with Millennials. Music consumes on average 2-6 hours of the Millennials day (Generation Z reports approximately 3 hours a day[26]), and in survey after survey Millennials and Generation Z identify music as an activity done with friends, for relaxation, for entertainment and for other social contexts[27]. The language of music is essentially the language of Millennials and Generation Z's social contexts. And the language that influences what words Millennials and Generation Z will use most often. And since music doesn't just convey language, it conveys values. This means that music is playing a fundamental role in the development of the language and values of individuals and the culture. It is not only reflecting values it is promoting and defining them, by shaping the language of the culture and individuals within the culture.

This observation adds more context to the argument for Taylor Swift's "Shake it Off" shaping culture. Taylor Swift's "Shake it Off" could potentially influence the overall culture, by shaping the idiolects of individuals, causing them to use the language of the Hater Mindset more often. This usage by individuals leads to an increased usage of the language in the culture. And since language is connected to meaning and worldview, this in turn shapes the worldview of those individuals, who in turn shape the worldview of the culture. Thus by doing so "Shake it Off" functions not just as a reflection of existing cultural values, but it also plays a role in helping to shape them. And in this case, it is shaping them with the Hater Mindset.

So is the Hater Mindset actually pervasive? A YouTube count of Taylor Swift's "Shake it Off" in April 2017 showed that the song had been viewed 2,048,535,462 times. In each of the 2 billion views of "Shake it Off" listeners were potentially having their embrace of the Hater Mindset echoed back to them or being shaped by the values present in the language of the song. And this is only Swift's "Shake it Off" song on YouTube. This says nothing of other musical artists, movies, TV shows, internet posts etc. also promoting the Hater Mindset themes. Even if it was the case, that only half the individuals who heard the YouTube version of "Shake It Off" were being impacted by the Hater Mindset that is still potentially 1 billion people exposed to the Hater Mindset. So in response to the question is the Hater Mindset actually pervasive, I would say yes it is extremely pervasive.

Chapter 3 – Inception: The Hater Mindset Version

"Even the smallest seed of an idea can grow. It can grow to define or destroy you.
- Dom Cobb from the movie Inception

This brings us to proposition 4 of the Taylor Swift argument. Answering the question of "how". How did the Hater Mindset become so pervasive? This answer takes us into the idea of the subconscious and implicit acceptance of the Hater Mindset. Before engaging with this proposition, I want to acknowledge that I know this is potentially the most controversial proposition of the Taylor Swift argument. Wading into any discussion on the subconscious can be problematic. The subconscious by its very nature is mysterious and prone to inordinate links between information and thought. Researchers who venture into what they see as a clear pool of coherent ideas on the subconscious often find themselves drowning in what turns out to be the murky swamp infested cesspool of convoluted and complicated thought. Recognizing this from the outset I will endeavor to engage this topic with great care and what may seem at times to be an overabundance of scholarly support. However, as I see this point as key to understanding why the Hater Mindset is pervasive in the culture, it is important that I take the plunge into the potential swamp that is the discussion of the subconscious.

The idea that music (and other media by extension) is subconsciously affecting individuals, or more precisely that it may be affecting *you*, is not an idea people tend to accept at face value. And it is bound to

47

provoke dissenters who don't want to view themselves as having parts of their thinking controlled by media. Most people believe themselves immune to any media, having any effect on their cognitive processes without their permission. And certainly don't believe it has a subconscious effect. However, as a brief counter example to this belief, and hopefully a way to make you less resistant to the next few pages, think about how often you get a song "stuck" in your head and can't get it out. Or for a more salient example see if you can finish this sentence "the best part of waking up…" If you said, "is Folgers in your cup" I would argue two things. One, you most likely sang the rest of the jingle, even if you did it in your head. And two, you probably never sat down with note cards, a notebook, and a highlighter to study the Folgers jingle. So your acquisition of the jingle happened subconsciously and without your permission. Having a song "stuck" in your head and memorizing a Folgers jingle are just two examples of how music, media, and the language used around you have the potential, and often do, work on your mind at the subconscious level.

The idea that the Hater Mindset is accepted subconsciously is important because this implicit and subconscious acceptance of the mindset explains its perpetuation. It should be clear by now that my vantage point on the Hater Mindset, paints it as a stroke of error on the canvas that is culture. This depiction of the mindset as negative though, creates at least one problem for my assertion. I am proposing that not only is the Hater Mindset negative it is pervasive. These two ideas should actually stand in stark contrast to each other. Items that are identified as flawed, dangerous, or detrimental are not usually perpetuated; they are halted, destroyed, or ceased. In 2014 Toyota Car Company made national news because of a recall of 1.7 million vehicles for a "range of defects"[1]. Through customer reports, internal research, and news outlets the company recognized a flaw in the configuration and construction of the braking system in their vehicles. In light of this revelation the company did not continue to use the flawed braking system or continue installing it into new vehicles. This would be an absurd and some would argue stupid approach to their situation. Toyota instead recalled the vehicles with the flawed system and ceased production on the problematic items. Toyota's actions provide an example of how most flawed and dangerous items are handled. They are eliminated. And this is usually the case when those flawed items are ideas as well. In her wonderful book on error *Being Wrong: Adventures in the Margin of Error* Kathryn Schulz lays out numerous examples of historic error that are no longer passed down or perpetuated in contemporary society[2]. One idea in particular is the idea that the Earth is the center of the universe, which was disproven by Galileo around 1632[3]. Currently, I know of no credible scholar who still holds to the geocentric or Earth centered view of the universe. The reason, is that this idea was shown to be flawed and thus was not preserved or disseminated further. Similarly, I know of no individuals who are currently ardent advocates for the argument that Milli and Vanilli were the best singers of the 90's either (if you don't know who Milli and Vanilli are, you were most likely born in the late 90's or 2000's or high for most of the 90's, please get to a computer and start googling immediately). My point is that the idea of discarding and eliminating flawed items is not limited to products, but can also be demonstrated in terms of ideas. And therein lies the paradox with our current discussion. If indeed the Hater Mindset is flawed, than why hasn't it been halted, destroyed, or ceased. If it is truly flawed this would seem to be the natural course of action for it. The fact that I am arguing that it has not been destroyed but is instead pervasive, I believe leaves two options for its continued existence. The first option is that the mindset is not flawed, that instead I am wrong. I believe at this point, it is probably clear that I do not believe this to be the preferred option. And I hope in the following chapters to show that the Hater Mindset is indeed flawed. In my mind, this leaves one other option, and that option is that the Hater Mindset is being disseminated at a subconscious and implicit level. Its perpetuation and acceptance is occurring at a level that is not consciously visible to most individuals. They are being "inceptioned" to borrow a term from the 2010 hit film "Inception". The Hater Mindset is being subconsciously disseminated and like the quote said at the beginning of this chapter, the seeds of the Hater Mindset are growing to define and destroy the culture.

To understand how this could occur I once again return back to the idea of language and its shaping of culture. As Boroditsky points out "changing how people talk changes how they think"[4]. Language shapes how individuals view the world, what they believe, and the ideas they hold. However, this process may not always occur on the conscious level. Often times this process is occurring on a level not known to the person who is utilizing the given language, or the individual whose views, ideas, worldview, and beliefs are being shaped by the language. In her 1996 work, *A Framework for Understanding Poverty* Dr. Ruby Payne outlines a model for how this *subconscious* process of language shaping belief and worldview occurs in reality[5]. She does this by proposing the idea of language and hidden class rules.

In her book on poverty Payne argues that there are hidden rules that govern behavior for different economic levels. She classifies these levels as poverty, middle class, and wealth, and argues that each of these levels have different rules for how an individual within those levels is expected to behave. She calls these the hidden rules of class, and writes "hidden rules are the unspoken cues and habits of a group"[6]. Payne identifies several areas where these rules affect behavior and value differently between economic classes. Areas such as love, worldview, money, social emphasis, time, and more are viewed differently by each group. She then proceeds throughout her text to paint an interwoven picture between language and the rules of economic class. Payne proposes that there are five registers of language. These include, the formal, consultative, casual, intimate, and frozen. Although Payne's engagement with these topics is thorough and important, for brevity sake, I will not define them here. What is of note from Payne's engagement with these topics is that the formal register is the register that is used in schools and businesses. Schools and businesses she argues function according to the hidden class rules associated with the formal register, which are the hidden middle class rules. These registers and rules are not formally taught to members of these economic levels but are learned implicitly. That is, that the language used around these individuals facilitates and forms what they value in the world and how they behave, subconsciously. Two of Payne's examples I found to be exceptionally true in my own life. Those are the areas of worldview and money.

Payne argues that in the category of worldview, people in poverty tend to see the world in terms of local settings and discuss events and news in these terms. Those from the middle class see the world in terms of a national setting, and discuss events and news in these terms. And individuals from the wealth economic level view the world internationally and this is reflected in their language and discourse. Payne argues that these views are not formally taught but are a reflection of an individual's primary discourse, or the language they first acquired from their setting. As I looked back at my life I found

51

Payne's example about those in poverty to be exceptionally relevant for my life. Growing up, for most of my life, my family and I would easily have been classified in Payne's poverty economic level. As an illustration I can recall one time in elementary school watching as some kids were attempting to "crack" (otherwise known as "playing the dozens" or "making fun of") on another kid. There "crack" went something like this "you so dumb you tried to get change from food stamps". Whether it was because I was far too young to understand what kind of self-disclosure would occur from my statement or because I just liked to show people what I knew, I immediately jumped in with confidence to state, "you *do* get change from food stamps". I knew this from firsthand experience. What is worse is that I was probably 12 years old before I recognized why they had all looked at me weirdly. I do want to pause here to say that my parents did a wonderful job raising me, and I do not tell this story or any other as a way to prop myself up, or diminish the hard work, love, peace, and fulfillment my parents provided for me throughout my life. I share it just to provide some context for my personal experience with language and hidden rules of class.

Growing up in Payne's poverty level I often talked about news in terms of local settings. What happened down the street, which one of my friends were in trouble, and other similar examples. I wasn't ever formally or consciously taught that the world was primarily local, but it was something I picked up from the way news and the world was discussed among my friends, peers, and environment. My forming of this worldview was implicit and subconscious. And it continued even into college. It wasn't until my first year of college that the language I found myself immersed in changed. As Payne points out, the language of schools is the formal register governed by the middle class rules. People in these settings view the world nationally. This was my experience during my first semester of college, and it was definitely a culture shock. A few weeks into my first semester of college I arrived at school one day and entered my first class to hear the professor say, "if anyone needs to take a break or leave in light of what happened today, please feel free." My mind raced. "What happened today? Was there a shooting? Did a student fall in the stairwell? What, what had happened?" The time was around 10:30 am and I had not heard of anything happening. The answer to my question was that there had been a terrorist attack in New York City. Two planes had flown into the World Trade Center Twin Towers, collapsing them. Hundreds of people had been killed, with many more missing or injured. I was in shock. Not from what had happened, my worldview at the time had not been expanded enough to understand the gravity of 9/11. I still thought of events as local and felt disconnected from larger national events. I was shocked that everyone knew what had transpired, and were profoundly affected by something that I did not even know had happened yet. Over the next few weeks I was inundated and overwhelmed with conversations about the nation, and the impact of 9/11. People all throughout campus were discussing it. I heard conversations in classrooms, hallways, courtyards, everywhere. The worldview of those at my college was different than my own; it was national as opposed to local. Soon after 9/11, I began to find myself scanning newspapers and articles each day wanting to understand the impact of events at the national level. I searched every day to learn about the conversations that were being had by government leaders, military actions that were occurring, and whatever other information I could get my hands on. Without recognizing how I had changed or my worldview had shifted, I began to view the world nationally. The language that was used around me had altered my view of the world but not consciously. It had been done on a subconscious level, subconsciously and implicitly. This is just one way that I recognized that the language used around me could shape my view of the world without my conscious awareness. I myself was "inceptioned". And this is what I am arguing occurs with the Hater Mindset.

A second area where I found Payne's work on language and hidden rules to be exceptionally relevant to my personal experience was in the area of money. Payne argues that economic levels also have hidden rules about the way in which money is viewed and utilized. Payne argues that for the individuals in the economic level of poverty, money is to be used or spent. For those in the middle class money is to be managed, and for those with wealth money is to be conserved or invested. It is important to note that Payne acknowledges that the hidden rules are generalizations and there are always exceptions. But her ideas provide a general framework. When I was made aware of Payne's work, I was working as a higher education professional at a community college in the Midwest. On this day I was in a workshop and a colleague was sharing Payne's concepts on the hidden rules around money. This was my first exposure to Payne's concepts and my first recognition that I had transitioned into a different set of hidden rules in this category. Without much explanation I was able to immediately conjure instances where I had seen Payne's rules play out in my own life. I could remember experiences where individuals, who like myself, had come from lower levels of income, tended to show off the money they acquired. They bought new visible items to show that they had money. TV's, cars, and phones, are just a few examples of the purchases I would see made at tax time, or as I entered college during financial aid refund time (I ended up creating a presentation called what not to do with your refund check). Similarly, I was able to visualize the conversations that were constantly occurring around me in my new setting as a higher education professional. Conversations around 403B's and budgets. Individuals speaking specifically in the terms of managing money. And finally, I was able to see the distinct difference between those conversations and the conversations of an affluent mentor I had at the time. Who discussed joining him in investment ventures that included purchasing office buildings, malls, or other commercial properties. All these thoughts flashed through my mind. Then I turned my reflections on this subject to myself, and I began to see my own personal example of transition from the hidden rules of poverty to the hidden rules of the middle class.

The example that came to mind for me was my first car as a teenager. When I was 15 years old, recognizing that I would soon be driving I set out to secure a vehicle. My first car was a 1991 ford Taurus that I purchased from a family friend for $200. All of the windows in the car including the front and back windshield were broken out. The battery was dead and the engine needed a lot of work. But I knew that I had to get the car running. Not so that I could use it for transportation, but because I had purchased two 15-inch speakers and a 600-watt amplifier that I wanted to get wired up into the car. I was going to pair it with some internal lights that flashed when the bass played. And that way everyone would know that I was coming from a block away and see that "my ride was fly". I had adopted this mindset because this was the approach that my friends and peers at the time had. A car was not for transportation it was for display. You had to show that you had one. As a lower income teenager, having a car in itself was an accomplishment, but having one that was "laid" was a win. I had to show that I had the money to buy the car and "lay it out", because money's purpose was to be spent. This lesson was never formally taught to me, but the conversations of my friends and peers at the time had subconsciously shaped the way that I viewed money and specifically my car. Fast forward to me sitting in a room years later listening to my colleague discuss the hidden rules of money. I looked back and recognized that for several years now I had not thought about spending money as something that is supposed to be done with money. In fact, I hated spending money. I no longer thought spending money on a car was cool. I thought not having a car payment and instead paying your car payment to your savings account was cool. The purpose of money for me at that point was to be managed not spent. Spending was a necessary evil, not a preferred way of utilizing money. It was far more important to save money or to figure out how to decrease expenditures. These were the thoughts that I now had. At that moment I recognized that I had not been formally taught these ideas and beliefs either. I had adopted them just by nature of them being the prevalent ideas in the discourse and exchanges that were happening around me. I myself was impacted by the hidden middle class rules, silently, implicitly, and without my consent. I was "inceptioned".

Payne's concept of language and hidden rules demonstrates how the minds and ideals of an individual can be influenced subconsciously. And often times without the individual even knowing it had occurred. The question that remains is, can this same process occur through the exposure to music (and media)? If my argument is that "Shake it Off" and other media with the Hater mindset message is subconsciously shifting worldviews and mindsets, I must determine if music or other media can *subconsciously* shift the ideals and views of individuals and the culture in the same way that language can? The simple answer is yes. As referenced earlier music can play a key role in influencing culture through influencing the idiolects of individuals. However, this is not the whole story. The examples of a song being "stuck" in your head or the Folgers jingle described earlier illustrate how music (and other media) is actually uniquely qualified to affect our cognition subconsciously and shape our view of the world without our permission. And this is primarily because of the way that our brains process music. Emotionally and subconsciously.

One of the unique things about music is that it is everywhere. Donald Hodges, Director of the Music Research Institute offered a test as a way to show how prevalent music is in a culture. He challenged readers to go 24 hours without hearing any music, and to chronicle how much of their lives they would have to change to do so. If you have doubts about the prevalence of music in culture I would challenge you to try Hodges' experiment. What is interesting to note however, is that even though music is such an integral part of our everyday existence, we often progress through our day completely oblivious to its existence. We are so used to hearing music that it hardly seems out of place in any area or at any time. It is in restrooms, elevators, cars, offices, I'm playing music as I write this sentence currently. As a reverse to the experiment proposed by Hodges, I would challenge readers to play music throughout the day for 24 hours and see how often the people you interact with perceive it as being out of place.

The reason that music can be everywhere and not be seen as a nuisance or bother is that "most of the processes involved in hearing and comprehending music are implicit and unconscious"[7]. Meaning that your brain processes music even if you are never aware that the process is happening. If music is present, your brain's subconscious processes become active and interact with the music on a subconscious and implicit level. Dr. Lars Heslet explains that the brain is split into three primary parts. The primitive brain, the middle brain, and the new brain. According to Heslet the brain processes music in all three of these parts simultaneously[8]. It engages the parts of our brain that deal with mind and space, and "has an effect on the subconscious"[9]. There is not one part of your brain that has sole control of music processing and thus there are underlying processes of music engagement going on each time you hear music. This is why you can learn the words to songs that you never even knew that you heard (Folgers jingles), or why some individuals find it hard to sleep with music on. Because of the way the brain processes music, even if you are unconscious there is still activity occurring in the brain if music is playing. Your brain processes music subconsciously.

It is important that a distinction be made here, unconscious or subconscious processing does not mean less impactful processing. It would be easy to hear the above argument made in reference to music and decide that just because the brain is processing music, doesn't mean that it is actually affecting the way an individual thinks. And while I believe this argument has been addressed with the earlier discussions of language and the shaping of culture, music has been shown to have a special relationship with one part of the cognitive process that is vitally important to shaping the way a person thinks. Music adds emotional charge to memory, which is essential to the formation of the way a person thinks. This point is summarized succinctly in a quote from Megan Cassano in her 2005 article written for the Journal of Heart-Centered Therapies. Cassano wrote:

> Music has the capacity of evoking various emotions based on lyrics or sound. When listening to music, people have a tendency to

apply the lyrics that they hear to their own lives…When an individual hears a song with lyrics that are applicable to his or her life, the subconscious mind records the feelings that are summoned by the song. This happens without any conscious awareness on the person's part.[10]

In this quote, Cassano lays out the reason that music has the capacity to cause people to subconsciously accept the Hater Mindset. It is because of the connection between music, emotion, and memory.

Music, Emotion, and Memory

It has been well established that memory and emotion are linked together. Some psychologists and philosophers even argue that human beings identities are an amalgam of their memories and the emotions connected to them. The researcher Elise Donovan explains it this way:

"our memory preserves us and who we are and where we have been, furnishes our sense of self, and is a combination of happy moments and shameful acts. To be ourselves we cannot abandon or forget who we once were"[11].

Without memory a person has no sense of identity or no basis on which to have a worldview, ideals, or beliefs. Thus at a very basic level the foundation of our worldview, ideals, and beliefs are our memories. However, it isn't just the memories alone. Our memories are indivisible from our emotions. We don't just remember events; we remember how we felt during those events. Think about your first love, or your first kiss, or the first time someone checked "yes" on your do you like me note (thank you Priscilla Gonzalez 3rd grade). You don't just remember the events you remember how you felt during the event. Emotion plays a key part in the retention and impact of memory. Studies have shown that "adrenal hormones and adrenergic signals are released in response to emotionally arousing events. These hormones then interact to facilitate memory formation, consolidation, and recall"[12]. This means that memories that are emotionally charged are more firmly cemented in the mind.

Recent research has caused some scholars to have doubt about the strength of the relationship between memory and emotion. However, it is important to note that this research has been conducted on accuracy of memory and not emotional impact. Historically it has been generally accepted that when an event occurs that is emotionally charged it is more likely to be cemented into the mind of an individual. One of the strongest recent examples used in psychology to illustrate this point are holocaust survivors. Even though the events experienced by Holocaust survivors occurred decades ago, many of them still recount these experiences in great detail. The proposed rationale behind why they are able to do this is that these events were emotionally impactful to those experiencing them and this increases the likelihood of those memories being imprinted firmly and vividly in the mind of the survivors. Similar examples have been used for individuals involved in dangerous criminal scenarios, military scenarios, and trauma situations.

Recently however, the work of researchers such as Elizabeth Loftus and others have started to cast doubt on human memory in general and by extension the generally accepted idea that emotionally charged memories are more firmly imprinted in the mind.[13] Through several experiments Loftus and her team have been able to convince individuals to have memories of events that never occurred. Or to describe events differently based on the language of the prompts given to them. And while I find Loftus, and similar scholars, work in this field fascinating it is important to note that their work is on memory accuracy and not on emotional impact. An individual may not remember accurately the events or details of a memory, but they can usually remember how they felt from the event. This feeling is what actually shapes the individuals identity and views, not the details of the event. In terms of changing the way a person believes and thinks, accuracy is not as important as feeling.

To provide some perspective relevant to the Taylor Swift discussion I offer my own experience. I don't actually remember the details of the room or what I was wearing the day that I first heard "Shake it Off". If someone were to quiz me on the size of the room, number of people present, or the color of the walls I would probably fail miserably. But what I do remember vividly and without question is how I felt about the words I was hearing. I felt like I needed to talk about what was going on in this song. I felt like the song was representative of a much larger issue in culture. And I felt like I knew I wanted to do something about it. The details of the event were not as important as the feelings evoked from the experience. The feelings are what led me to change my way of thinking and write this book. This is the role that music plays in terms of memories and emotions. It evokes emotion around memory cementing the feelings of that memory in the mind. And this is often done at the subconscious level.

In their 2001 *Handbook of Music and Emotion,* Patrik Justin and John Sloboda write that music affects emotions both actively and passively[14]. That is that it affects emotions when people are aware of it and when they are not aware of it. Other scholars have also found this to be true. In one study participants listened to happy music and sad music. The study found that happy music caused more cheekbone and facial muscle activity, and higher levels of happiness than did sad music. The authors concluded that our bodies respond to music subconsciously, and it can affect our emotions.[15] One of my favorite examples of the link between emotion, music, memory, and the subconscious is provided by Megan Cassano. Cassano uses the example of how movies and TV shows will often choose a song to accompany a particularly sad scene. Later when an individual hears that song, they will often experience feelings of sadness, even if it is years later. Cassano states that this is because "when feelings enter conscious awareness, the subconscious mind creates a memory based on what is happening"[16], and music can be used to provoke those feelings. The person may have no conscious recall of the movie, but they are still aware of the feelings the song provoked. Thus again supporting the idea that what impacts individuals is not the details of the memory but the feelings surrounding it, and this process is often subconscious.

Recognizing that music is processed through implicit and subconscious processes, as well as acknowledging music's ability to emotionally charge memories with feelings that become firmly cemented in the mind, helps to answer the question of whether music (or other media) can indeed shape an individual's ideals, values and worldview subconsciously. The answer is yes. And if music can do this, it can certainly transmit the Hater Mindset subconsciously. And the subconscious transmission of the Hater Mindset answers the question of how the Hater Mindset became pervasive. The reason that the flawed mindset has not been ceased, halted, or destroyed is because it is transmitted and promulgated subconsciously and implicitly.

Summary

It is customary in many of my favorite books for the author to put a quote by a well- known person at the beginning of each chapter. This quote is used as a way to provoke thought in the reader but also to provide a foreshadowing of where the chapter is going to go. The quote I placed at the beginning of chapter 2 was "Haters" and it is attributed to "everyone, everywhere". While I don't know if this is thought provoking or written by a well-known person, I do hope it provided a foreshadowing for the direction of the next two chapters. The idea that the word "hater" is used by everyone everywhere, while it may be hyperbole, also speaks to the pervasiveness of the word and its associated mindset in our culture. I began this chapter by stating that in 2014 I began saying a statement that most people would think was outrageous. It was centered on the idea of Taylor Swift being the most dangerous person in the world. For me this danger was based on her role in the pervasiveness of the Hater Mindset. And throughout these two chapters I have endeavored to examine the pervasiveness of this mindset, by using Taylor Swift as the model. I used proposition 1 of my argument to answer the question of why it matters if the Hater Mindset is pervasive. I used propositions 2 and 3 of my argument to answer the question if the Hater Mindset was indeed truly pervasive. And I used proposition 4 of the argument to show how the Hater Mindset became so pervasive in society. Having now transgressed topics from linguistics and psychomusicology, to Jay-Z/Nas rap battles and my first car. I hope that you have gotten a better sense of me and why I felt the need to write this book. With this groundwork now laid, I invite you to join me as we jump into the examination of the effects of the Hater Mindset within individuals and the culture. And accompany me on the journey I hope will lead you to "BE A HATER".

PART 2- "HATER"

Chapter 4 – Why you always dissenting…Hater?

"I Dissent"
- *Ruth Bader Ginsburg T-Shirt*

As discussed earlier, the structure of this book is arranged as an analysis of the statement, "You are just a hater". The obvious approach to the examination of the "you are just a hater" sentence would be to begin the analysis at the beginning with the word "you" and continue in reading order down the sentence. This is of course how people read and it would make logical sense to approach the sentence in the same way that people read. However, I do not plan to do this. The problem with taking this approach is that it would leave the most prominent part of the "you are just a hater" sentence, the word "hater", until the end, And while the word "hater" is found at the end of the "you are just a hater" sentence it clearly serves as the pièce de résistance of the phrase. It is the apex of the sentence and the word whose presence projects meaning into the preceding words. Without the word "hater", the sentence's meaning could and would be altered or diminished. A simple exercise in substitution demonstrates this point. If I were to say "you are just a…genius" or "you are just …a lover" the implications and meaning of the "you are just a hater" sentence change dramatically. Similarly, if I were to substitute more spiteful words like "you are just a … joke", or "you are just a … loser" for example, the tone of the sentence would change due to the new ending words. The usage of the words "loser" or "joke" mirror the usage of the word "hater", in that they are also designed to diminish another individual. But they seem to hold a much more offensive contextual tone. Most often these sentences are seen as especially malicious while "you are just a hater" is not. Think about how you would feel if someone called you a joke or a loser. You would probably be much more offended than if they called you a "hater". The words "loser" and "joke" in reference to individuals has not been absorbed into the culture the way hater has, so that when you hear someone call another person a loser or a joke you are likely to view these sentences as hurtful and harmful. Their usage and associated meanings have not been engrained into the normal vocabulary of the culture like hater has. So to hear "loser" or "joke" spoken in reference to another individual may still provoke an emotional or even visceral response. While typically, hearing someone called a hater does not evoke the same emotion. Even though I would argue the phrase "you are just" in itself has potentially serious implications that should most likely be avoided (this will be discussed later), the inclusion of the word "hater" at the end of the phrase is what makes the "you are just a hater" sentence worth examining. For me this is certainly not "a rose by any other name" situation. And since that is the case I have chosen to begin my examination of the phrase "you are just a hater" at the end with the word "hater".

Yet, even though I am confident that this is where the analysis should begin, this confidence does not relieve the sense of hesitation I have about beginning. I feel much like the man who is challenged to eat an elephant. The sheer magnitude of the task in front of him being so daunting, that he says to his friend:

> Man: How do I begin to eat this elephant?
> Friend: The only way you can.
> Man: How is that?
> Friend: One bite at a time. It is easy… Unless…
> Man: Unless what?
> Elephant: Unless I don't want to be eaten.

My similarities with the man in the story can be seen in three different ways. The first is that I, like he, am facing a large and daunting task in the word "Hater". It is such a simple word, its composition holding less letters than my first name (my full name is Weston). But the magnitude of "hater" is not in its letters, it is in the meaning constructed through them when they are assembled together in the specified order, h-a-t-e-r. The meaning that has implications for critical thinking, epistemic motivation, learning, innovation, curiosity, and more. Many of which I plan to deal with in the next chapter. The undertaking of engaging with this topic is to me what the elephant was to the man in the story, massive. The second way that I see myself reflected in the man in the story is that I am also endeavoring to address a large topic in small bite size pieces. Many of my observations on the Hater Mindset are derived from, and relevant to, my personal areas of research and interest. This research covers multiple areas of cognitive thinking, reasoning, and psychology and incorporates theory from numerous fields. And because I am passionate about these topics this book could easily be extended into a several hundred page long volume allowing me to publicly cogitate on the link between organizational psychology, organizational leadership, performance, innovation and the Hater Mindset. But, much like the story of the man eating the elephant, this would probably only be an enjoyable experience for one of us, namely me. My goal instead, is to offer bite sized elements of analysis that can be utilized in the "real world" beyond academia. To provide cursory understandings of theory without delving into the depths of the topics. The third way that I feel the man in the story's situation mirrors my own is more simplistic, but just as important. And that is that we are both dealing with dissent. His interaction with dissent comes in the form of the elephant that objects to being eaten and mine comes from one of the core beliefs of the Hater Mindset. The dismissal and disdain of dissent. While his interaction with dissent may have dire consequences for him physically (and with the fact that the elephant spoke, probably emotionally as well), my interaction with dissent has implications for the current culture and the future of dissent within it.

Dissent of course being the academic term for "hating". Which of course is the verb form of "hater" from the root word "haterandi hateramas". (Actually I made that bit about the root word up, just wanted to make sure you are still paying attention). Dissent is key when truly setting out to examine the Hater Mindset. The dictionary defines dissent as "to differ in sentiment or opinion"[1]. That is, to have a point of view that differs from someone else's. Even a cursory reading of the definition of dissent reveals its similarity with the definition of a hater proposed in chapter 1.

A person who holds a position, opinion, view, or perspective that is different from the position, opinion, view, or perspective that you currently hold.

This hater definition essentially defines a hater as someone who "differs in sentiment or opinion" or in other words someone who dissents. So while in contemporary society a person may be labeled a hater, in the field of organizational psychology and academia that person is simply expressing dissent. (As a side note you now have a sly way to reply the next time someone calls you a hater. You can tell them you are not hating you just dissent from their opinion). In current culture the idea of a hater and the concept of dissent have been conflated together. And the issue with the conflation of dissent and the concept of a hater, is that this conflation leads to a dismissal and disdain for dissent in general. Which is the first implication of the Hater Mindset. It leads people to disdain and dismiss dissent.

As I mentioned above people love to hate haters. As a culture we write songs about hating haters, we post on Facebook about hating haters, we love to hate haters. I once saw a t-shirt that on the front read "I LOVE TO HATE" and on the back it read "HATERS". So with this hatred for haters, it would only make sense that anything that is conflated with hating or haters would be hated too. (I know that sentence had a lot of hate in it). Thus, when being a hater is conflated with dissent, what begins to happen is that people begin to hate dissent the same way that they hate haters. All dissent becomes hating and all dissenters become haters. Both of which are hated in contemporary society. This approach is problematic for many reasons but I will focus on one reason in particular. The fact that dissent has actually been shown to be quite beneficial for society, organizations, cultures, and for individuals as well.

In my opinion, one of the strongest cases made for the need for dissent was written by Cass Sunstein. Sunstein, who is often called the most cited law professor in the country, wrote a book entitled *Why Societies Need Dissent*[2]. In his book Sunstein offers several arguments for the need for dissent and the importance of dissent to societies. These arguments range from the need for dissent as a way to improve decisions and decision making, to the need for dissent as a way to counter negative information cascades. Sunstein's focus in the book is the need for dissent at a societal level, but much of his commentary is also beneficial to understanding dissent at the cultural and individual level. Which is where the focus and emphasis of this book lies, on dissent and the Hater Mindset at the cultural and individual level.

One of the most salient points Sunstein makes

71

that is relevant to the discussion of the Hater Mindset, is his distinction of different types of dissent. Sunstein distinguishes between at least two different classifications of dissent, "disclosing dissent" and "contrarian dissent". Disclosing dissent according to Sunstein is dissent that shares or reveals information that was not previously provided in the discourse or situation. It is essentially dissent that adds new perspective and information into the discourse or situation. Sunstein invokes the example of the little boy in the "Emperor's New Clothes" short story as an example of a discloser. For those unfamiliar with the story, it consists of two tailors who tell an Emperor that they will make him a special set of clothes. The clothes will be invisible to anyone who is either stupid, incompetent, or unfit for their position. When the Emperor goes to receive his "new clothes", he is unable to see them. Out of fear that he will be labeled unfit for his position, the Emperor dons the new "clothes", and proceeds in a processional before his subjects. The Emperor's subjects and advisors also refuse to acknowledge that they cannot see the clothes for fear that they will be labeled stupid or incompetent. As the Emperor is marching in a processional, the members of the kingdom are remaining silent and playing along until a little boy shouts out that the Emperor isn't wearing anything at all. It is at this point that the crowd also begins to acknowledge the Emperor is not wearing any clothes. Sunstein invokes the child who points out the Emperor's nakedness in the story as an example of a discloser. According to Sunstein, disclosers should genuinely be prized. Their presence helps individuals and groups to make better decisions. As you would expect would invariably happen in the case of the Emperor and his clothes. You would expect that in the future he would make better decisions in terms of appearing before his subjects clothed. Unless of course he has *some other* proclivities not mentioned in the story (wink, wink). Disclosers also help to counter negative information cascades, just as the little boy in the story did. Negative information cascades are the spreading of flawed information to individuals and throughout a group. These cascades occur when no one speaks up to counter the negative or flawed information. In the story the crowd was able to counter the negative information being spread (the belief that the Emperor was actually wearing invisible clothes and they were too stupid, incompetent, or unfit for their positions to see it) after the boy practiced disclosing dissent. And they were also able to acknowledge and embrace better information due to the disclosing dissent of the little boy. Namely that the Emperor was in fact naked. Instead of further spreading information that was not correct, they countered the negative information cascade. The last thing that disclosing dissent does is that it offers a new perspective or view on information. One that may not have been considered before. In the case of the Emperor's New Clothes story it allowed the crowd to consider the alternative that they were not stupid or incompetent but that the Emperor himself simply had on no clothes. This was a perspective that was tenable but was not considered (at least publicly) until the disclosing dissent from the little boy occurred. It is these three reasons, better decision making, stopping negative information cascades, and offering alternative perspectives on situations that make disclosing dissent something that societies, organizations, cultures and individuals should value.

On the other hand, Sunstein also identifies a second type of dissent. This dissent he calls contrarian dissent. Contrarian dissent is when an individual dissents simply for the sake of disagreeing. They are contrary to the current perspective just for the sake of being contrary. People who practice this type of dissent are called contrarians. When speaking of contrarians Sunstein writes:

> *In many cases, contrarians are most unlikely to help the group. If the contrarian is known as such his statement will not be very informative. People will think "this is the sort of person who always disagrees with us" and the disagreement will not be helpful.*[3]

Sunstein goes on to say that a contrarian may offer good points at times simply because they will challenge conventional wisdom. This challenge to conventional wisdom may result in new perspectives being added to the dialogue. It is the "even a broke clock is correct twice a day idea". These individuals may occasionally add beneficial information and perspective to the group through their effort to be contrary. However, Sunstein's point is that when a contrarian is identified as such, his or her information will not be considered helpful or in many cases even paid attention to. This is because contrarians are considered an "other" group by most people. We will talk more about other groups in chapter 9. For now, it is important to note that the majority of people do not see themselves or even most other people as contrarians. People who *are* contrarians or practice contrarian dissent, are considered to be "others". They are not like most people and they are certainly not like "us". Thus they are "others". In addition to being "others", contrarians are considered to be "others" with an agenda. That agenda is to counter any perspective that comes forth regardless of merit or validity. Contrarian dissent emerges simply for the sake of dissenting, not to counter flawed thoughts or perspectives or to provide new ways of looking at things, but simply to dissent. This clarification is important because when it comes to dissent people are far less likely to take an "other" advocacy group or an "other" group with an agenda seriously. Sunstein points out that the dissenting opinions of groups perceived as "others" are far less convincing when those groups are suspected to have an agenda. Psychology has shown that this fact is increased even further when you are talking about contrarians. In group theory, a person who is characterized as disagreeing for the sake of disagreeing is usually associated with strong negative feelings and emotions by others. Their opinion's and views are less likely to be considered and they are likely to have lower levels of social capital (feelings of trust, loyalty, and value) from the group. Dissent from these individuals is usually met with disdain or dismissal.

I believe that it is the essence of contrarian dissent that is usually being imagined when someone calls someone else a hater. When someone calls another person a hater, what the labeler is implying is that the person they are calling a hater (the labeled person) has contrarian dissent. They are implying that the person is not dissenting as a way to offer new perspective or information, to improve decision-making, or to stop negative information cascades. In other words, they are not practicing disclosing dissent. Instead, when someone calls someone a hater, they are saying that the other person is dissenting simply for dissents sake. That they don't actually have merit or value in their perspective they are simply dissenting for the sake of dissenting. They are practicing contrarian dissent. And by imagining that contrarian dissent is the dissent of the "hater", the labeling individual is giving himself or herself permission to dismiss and disdain the information being presented. As Sunstein stated,

> *If the contrarian is known as such his statement will not be very informative. People will think*

"this is the sort of person who always disagrees with us" and the disagreement will not be helpful.[4]

And if the person's dissent is not helpful why pay attention to it at all. So while disclosing dissent is to be genuinely prized, contrarian dissent is usually met with disdain, dismissal, and the label of hating or hater.

The question that immediately arises from the distinction between disclosing dissent and contrarian dissent then is, when is dissent disclosing and when is it contrarian. What distinguishes disclosing dissent, the useful kind, from contrarian dissent, the useless kind? This is where Sunstein's distinction in terms becomes murky. The reason for the murkiness is that the distinction between whether dissent is disclosing or contrarian depends on the vantage point of the receiver of the dissent. An individual's internal cognitive processes determine whether the dissent they are hearing is disclosing or contrarian. There is actually a vivid example of how an individual's vantage point determines if what they are hearing is classified as dissent or hating, that has been playing out recently in the culture.

As of late, the term dissent has become more popular in pop culture, heralded by fans and supporters of Supreme Court Justice Ruth Bader Ginsburg and her fiery written dissents on Supreme Court decisions. There are countless stores throughout the country offering t-shirts and just as many memes online that read "I Dissent" next to the face of Justice Ginsburg. One of my favorites consists of Justice Ginsburg's picture with the words Notorious R.B.G. and "I dissent" written at the bottom. For fans and supporters of Justice Ginsburg it is obvious that she is a needed voice in the midst of contrary perspectives. She adds a new vantage point that helps make better decisions, counter negative information cascades, and provide alternative perspectives on issues. In essence, she practices disclosing dissent. However, the fandom and support offered for Justice Ginsburg also sheds light on the fact that one person's dissent is another person's "hater". While an internet search for "Justice Ginsburg meme" reveals countless fun memes of support for the dissents of Justice Ginsburg, it doesn't take more than a couple of clicks in a google search on Ruth Bader Ginsburg before you come across people dubbing Justice Ginsburg, Ruth "Hater" Ginsburg (not to be confused with the Roller Derby Star, who I'm sure also dissents from her opponents quite often). For these individuals Justice Ginsburg is not offering disclosing dissent instead she is just a "hater" and her dissents are simply her "hating". These individuals see Justice Ginsburg's dissents as liberal advocacy that will disagree with every decision. In this view, Justice Ginsburg practices contrarian dissent, or in other words she is just hating. This bifurcated view on the dissent of Justice Ginsburg elucidates the fact that the line between hater and dissent is based on an individual's current perspective. A person's perspective determines what kind of dissent they believe is occurring, disclosing or contrarian.

For me Sunstein's distinction between disclosing and contrarian dissent, and the understanding that the distinction between the two occurs in the mind of the dissent receiver, also exposes a vital component of the Hater Mindset. That component is that the Hater Mindset eliminates or at least dampens an individual's perception of dissent as disclosing and heightens the perception of dissent as contrarian. As I stated earlier when someone calls someone else a hater they are most likely imagining contrarian dissent. They believe the person is dissenting for the sake of dissenting. The Hater Mindset views most if not all dissent as contrarian instead of disclosing. It allows people to view any dissent as a person dissenting for the sake of dissenting. And thus anyone who has embraced the Hater Mindset (which I propose is *a lot* of people) reacts to dissent in general as if it is dissent being offered from a contrarian perspective. Instead of these individuals seeing the dissent or dissenter as something to be "genuinely prized", they react with dismissal, disdain, or hostility toward dissent. Instead of engaging with the dissenter as someone offering a different perspective, helping him or her to think differently, or helping them to make a better decision, they label them a "hater". It is important that I state here that I do not believe this is being done intentionally. That these individuals are consciously speaking to themselves about the two types of dissent (that would be some intense metacognition). But just like stated in chapter 3, I believe the perception of dissent as contrarian instead of disclosing is being done subconsciously and implicitly. Most individuals are not even aware that this is how they view dissent. And the larger cultural challenge is that a continued practice of viewing all dissent as contrarian and labeling all dissent as hate, and all dissenter's as haters leads to a detrimental outcome for societies and individuals.

Sunstein argues that a society that is unchecked by dissent "can produce disturbing, harmful, and sometimes astonishing outcomes"[5].These include the rise of tyrants, the loss of free speech, poorer decisions, negative information cascades, group think, and even cruelty to other human beings. Sunstein provides several examples from the Bay of Pigs where despite several people in the government knowing it was a mistake, the US made a massive military blunder invading Cuba. To the Stanford Prison Experiments where a researcher named Philip Zimbardo placed normal individuals in the roles of prisoners or guards in a mock prison. In a matter of days the experiment had to be shut down because of the cruelty of the "guards" and the decaying health of the "prisoners". More recent examples include Abu Ghraib prison where guards failed to dissent from their supervisors and it lead to the torturous treatment of prisoners. Or the story of Matthew Carrington who had a seizure and later died after an extreme hazing session by his fraternity brothers. None of them called the police for fear of dissenting from the other fraternity brothers. In each of these cases a lack of dissent was shown to have profound consequences. The debrief from the failed Bay of Pigs military invasion revealed that those with doubts about the mission were afraid to offer their disagreement for fear of repercussions. And thus they remained silent and did not express their dissent to the course of action taken, which led to deadly consequences. In the case of the Stanford Prison Experiments, none of the "guards" dissented from the other "guards" about the way they were treating the volunteer "prisoners" and the experiment had to be quickly shut down due to their cruelty. Abu Ghraib prisoners faced torture, rape, sodomy, and even murder because none of the guards wanted to dissent from their supervisors. And Matthew Carrington had a seizure and lost his life in front of his fraternity brothers because none of them wanted to express dissent.

One of the most striking examples offered by Sunstein about the negative outcomes birthed out of an absence of dissent is the Milgram experiments[6]. The Milgram experiments consisted of a study conducted by a psychologist named Stanley Milgram in the 1960's. In this study Milgram asked subjects to administer electric shocks to a person who was located in an adjoining room. The subjects were told that the purpose of the study was to examine the effect of punishment on memory. The subjects were asked to shock the person in the other room for incorrect answers with voltage levels that ranged from 15 to 450. These voltage levels were also marked with accompanying words from "slight shock" to "XXX". The subjects were asked by a person they believed to be the lead researcher to turn the voltage of the shock up for each wrong answer given. Luckily in Milgram's experiment both the "shocks" and the "patient" receiving them were fake. The reason this is lucky is because the patient who was actually an actor continued to give wrong answers and the "lead researcher", also an actor, continued to request stronger shocks to the patient. These requests went well into the voltage levels that were clearly marked as dangerous. In the end, 100% of the participants continued to obey the researcher even into the dangerously marked levels. This lack of dissent occurred regardless of occupation (engineers, teachers, postal clerks) or age (20-50). Milgram likened the behavior of the subjects in the study to the behavior of Germans under Nazi rule. And Sunstein argues that the Holocaust and the rise of Nazism are just potential examples of outcomes that can arise when societies don't allow dissent. They serve as examples of how quickly and profoundly a dismissal and disdain for dissent can impact societies.

The examples in Sunstein's book serve as warning posts for what happens when societies, governments, and even nations move to dismiss and disdain dissent. Societies need dissent in order to flourish, and without it Sunstein argues they may face dire negative consequences. But while Sunstein examines a dismissal and disdain for dissent at the societal level, this book is about the impact of the dismissal and disdain of dissent at the cultural and individual level. This begs the question are the stakes just as high when dismissal and disdain for dissent are done at the individual level. If I am arguing that the Hater Mindset is pervasive, leads to a dismissal and disdain for dissent, and eventually the labeling of individuals as haters, how does that affect culture and individuals? What happens to an individual when they form a habit of engaging dissent with disdain or dismissal? And to the culture when it follows suit? What impact does it have on an individual to label people who dissent from them "haters"? And what happens to a culture when this approach is pervasive in the individuals of that culture? It is to these questions that I now turn. So while it was the scholar Sunstein who helped to classify the two types of dissent and to illuminate the effect of dismissal and disdain for dissent on a societal level, to examine the impact of dismissal and disdain for dissent on an individual level we turn to a more recent sage and scholar, the rapper GUCCI MANE.

Chapter 5 – Cognitive Psychology with GUCCI MANE

"I'm not listening, I'm not interested.
My attention only focused on what I get"
- Gucci Mane "Haterade Lyrics"

It would be easy to assume based on the title of this chapter, the title of chapter 2, and the musical references throughout this book that I listen to a lot of popular music. The truth is that my musical preferences would more accurately be described as "underground" than popular (Street Hymns, or Serge anyone?). However, as was discussed in chapter 2 the popular music of a society plays a uniquely dichotomous role in relation to that society's culture. The popular music of a society helps to shape the culture of that society by shaping the language and values of the culture and the individuals within it. It also serves as a mirror and manifesto for the prominent ideas and values that are present in that culture as well. So for me, an examination of a cultural phenomenon like the Hater Mindset would naturally include an analyses of popular music. A cultural observer can learn a lot about a culture and the values of that culture by engaging with the popular music of that culture. In chapter 2 I used the example of Taylor's Swift's "Shake it Off" to illustrate this connection between ideas and values, and their reflection in the popular music of culture. I looked specifically at the link between "Shake It Off" and the promulgation of the Hater Mindset. However, it is important to note that while I think Swift's "Shake it Off" can serve as the apex of the crescendo that is the Hater Mindset in culture, it was not the first song to be built around the concept of haters and certainly not the first to illustrate the Hater Mindset. In fact in 2014, the same year that "Shake it Off" hit the scene, the entertainment section of Time Magazine's website posted an article titled "Taylor Swift's Shake it Off and 7 other songs about Haters". The article written by Eliana Dockterman listed songs that ranged from 50 cent's "In Da Club" released in 2003 through Swift's "Shake it off" released in 2014[1]. That range of songs indicates at least a decade of songs about haters being written before "Shake it Off" came along. Some commentators argue the history is even longer and that "Playas Gon' Play" written by 3LW and released in 2001 served as the cultural singularity or origination point for the hater phenomenon. I personally support this idea because it would represent a sweet serendipitous history of the concept of haters in music. One where the chorus of the song that birth songs about haters, uses the lyrics "playas they gon play, and haters they gonna hate". And the song that I dubbed the apex of the crescendo of the Hater Mindset in culture "Shake It Off ",uses the lyrics "a players gonna play; and a haters gonna hate" in its chorus. The beautiful irony of this connection would be one I would love to see.

Regardless of whether my beautiful irony belief is correct or not, it is still apparent that songs about haters have been written for quite a while. And as such, there has been a plethora of thoughts and ideas penned, sang, written, and shared that discuss the Hater Mindset. Many of these songs offer profound insight into the effects of the Hater Mindset on culture and individuals within the culture. One such song was written in 2010 by the rap artist Gucci Mane. In 2010 with the help of Nicki Minaj and Pharrell Williams, Gucci Mane released the song Haterade on his *The Appeal: Georgia's Most Wanted* album. It is probably clear from the title of the song that the song took particular aim at "haters", as they are usually defined in contemporary culture, and illustrates aspects of the Hater Mindset. In the last chapter I argued that one of the core beliefs of the Hater Mindset is that it results in a disdain and dismissal of dissent. I concluded the chapter by stating that I wanted to examine the impact that this disdain and dismissal of dissent has on individuals. In Gucci Mane's "Haterade", we get a glimpse at the answers to the questions posed at the end of chapter 3. Specifically in the first three lines rapped by Gucci Mane during his verse of the song. Gucci Mane begins his verse stating

> *" I'm not listening.*
> *I'm not interested.*
> *My attention only focused on what I get."*

In these few lines, Gucci Mane offers a treatise on his approach to haters. His statements point to a disdain and dismissal of dissent for his "haters" and at the same time shed light on the effects that dismissal and disdain for dissent has on individuals and their thinking. These effects not only answer the questions posed at the end of chapter 3 but also illustrate the detrimental impact of these effects to the current culture and the individuals within it. In these three lines we learn that a dismissal and disdain for dissent (brought on by the Hater Mindset) leads individuals to *not listen*, which makes them less likely to of be critical thinkers. To *not be interested* which hinders their learning. And to only *focus their attention* on what they get, which leads to lower levels of epistemic motivation and higher levels of confirmation bias. By examining Gucci Mane's lyrics at the beginning of his verse, we get an in depth look into the cognitive psychology of individuals who have embraced the Hater Mindset.

I'm Not Listening

The first line of Gucci Mane's verse states, "I'm not listening". At the outset of his hypothetical discourse with those that he has determined are haters, Gucci Mane begins the conversation by ending half of it. He wants it to be unequivocally known that he is not listening. Any perspective or viewpoints offered by the person speaking (the hater/dissenter) will not be given the courtesy of ear time with Gucci Mane. And since this hypothetical discourse is with a hater, we can only assume that the ideas and perspectives that Gucci Mane is refusing to hear differ from his own. This statement by Gucci Mane is an illustration of how people with the Hater Mindset choose to respond to dissent from "haters". They don't listen to it. Their dismissal and disdain for dissent is so strong that when faced with dissent, the Hater Mindset will choose not to listen to the dissent. And since a hater is anyone who holds a position or view different from the one an individual currently holds, what in essence happens is people will choose not listening as a way to deal with dissent in general. This is one of the first and major symptoms of the Hater Mindset. It causes individuals to respond to dissent by not listening. And the decision to not listen to dissent ultimately leads to an avoidance of cognitive dissonance and eventually results in a decline in critical thinking (more on this later).

The decision to "not listen" in response to dissent is actually an odd one. At first glance it may not seem like odd behavior. We have all known someone who took this approach, or even been the person that took this approach, to differing opinions at one point or another. In fact, I would argue with the rise of the Hater Mindset, this approach to dissent is actually the expected type of behavior in cases where people feel they are being "hated on" or more accurately "dissented from". The phrase "don't listen to them" often serves as an antecedent for calling someone a hater. "Don't listen to them, they are just haters". So at first glance it doesn't seem odd at all when Gucci Mane or anyone else takes the same approach because we have seen so many people choose to "not listen" as a way to cope with dissent. However, if we take a step back and use a more analytical perspective, the decision not to listen to dissent or "haters" does seem like an odd one doesn't it? *Not listening,* actually takes a lot of effort. Listening, at its core, is an almost effortless endeavor. It is often something that happens without us applying any conscious thought. In fact all of us can probably remember a time when we ended up listening to someone tell a story that we had no interest in at all. In our heads we were yelling at the person to shut-up, but still we listened, because it cost us nothing and took no effort. On the other hand, it often takes considerably *more effort not to listen*, than to listen. My daughters will often find themselves in a situation similar to Gucci Mane. One where they disagree with each other and don't want to listen to the other person. In order to stop themselves from listening they will stick their fingers in their ears and yell loudly so that they can't hear the other person talking. BLAH, BLAH, BLAH is their preferred phrase if you were wondering. While listening occurs passively and without effort, my daughters have to use two different actions (fingers in their ears, and yelling loudly) to effectively not listen. This is a lot of effort to simply avoid listening to a differing opinion and it seems it would actually be much easier to just listen. For me personally the amount of effort needed to avoid listening is exhausting. Why then do we do it? What is it that drives us from an effortless activity, listening, to apply so much effort *to not* listen? One answer to this question was offered by the psychologist Leon Festinger back in the 1960's. His answer is that people choose to not listen to dissenting ideas because they want to avoid cognitive dissonance. And avoiding cognitive dissonance, as it turns out, is actually the key component that causes not listening to lead to a decline in critical thinking.

The concept of cognitive dissonance is one of the most researched and recognized concepts in the field of psychology. The concept is grounded in the research Festinger conducted on understanding the way people think, specifically how they think about conflicting information. In 1962, Leon Festinger and his team infiltrated a California doomsday group called "the Seekers"[2]. The seekers believed that their leader Marion Keech was a prophet who received messages from the planet Clarion. Festinger and his team were interested in understanding how people dealt with information that differed from their existing beliefs. For Festinger and his team "The Seekers" were an exciting group to study because the beliefs of the group were specific. "The Seekers" believed the world was going to end on December 21st and a spaceship would arrive to rescue them. Festinger and his team recognized that if a doomsday event did not occur on December 21st "the Seekers" would be faced with a strong level of information that differed from their previously held beliefs and ideas. Ultimately, Festinger was correct. At the appointed time on December 21st nothing happened, no space ship came, and "the Seekers" were not rescued from a Doomsday event. However, something else happened that captured Festinger and his team's attention. When the proposed doomsday arrived and there was no spaceship, members of "the Seekers" did not immediately pack up their bags and go home having recognized their error. Instead, they first begin to look for anything that could have hindered their rescue. They removed additional clothing they believed tethered them to Earth, they took out fillings from their teeth, they even reset their watches (maybe they thought Clarion was on Hawaii Standard Time). When there was still no Clarion spaceship the group members did not abandon their beliefs and ideas. Instead, they stood around bewildered, as if in a mental fog. Festinger and his team reported that this fog persisted until eventually the leader of "The Seekers" stood before the group and reported to have one last message from Clarion. The message stated, "this little group, sitting all night long, has spread so much goodness and light that the God of the universe spared the Earth from destruction"[3].

Festinger's engagement with "The Seeker's" provided him with two key observations which eventually developed into his concept and theory of cognitive dissonance. These observations help to explain why people choose to avoid listening to dissenting views. Festinger's two observations were

1) Differing information or dissent leads to dissonance.
2) Dissonance creates a need/drive to return to consonance.

Festinger observed that when the Clarion ship did not appear "The Seekers" faced a sort of mental discomfort and anxiety. They did not just accept that their ideas were wrong. Instead they felt a tension with the new information provided (no spaceship) and what they believed (a spaceship would come). Festinger concluded that when individuals in general not just "The Seekers" hear, experience, learn, or engage with information that is different from cognitive information they already hold as true, it creates feelings of discomfort and senses of anxiety. These feelings Festinger called cognitive dissonance. The formal definition of Cognitive Dissonance is

> "a state of tension that occurs whenever an individual simultaneously holds two cognitions (ideas, attitudes, beliefs, opinions) that are psychologically inconsistent"[4].

You have probably seen this experience in others or faced it yourself. I remember one incidence in particular where I both saw cognitive dissonance in someone else and experienced in myself simultaneously.

As a person who wants to seek out dissent instead of dismiss it, I will often seek out what I call "dialogue partners". These "dialogue partners" are people who I know hold views different from mine on various subjects. In one particular experience with a dialogue partner (we'll call him Terry) I was able to not only recognize cognitive dissonance in Terry, but to recognize that I too was facing it. Terry and I had finished a pretty intense conversation on a topic in which we differed. Both of us left the conversation agreeing that we would think more about the opinions of the other person. A couple of days later Terry came into my office to tell me that he had been thinking about something I said. What struck me about this encounter was that while Terry was speaking, the brow of his forehead was wrinkled, and his face seemed tight. Not super tight or super wrinkled but just slightly tight and wrinkled. He had the look a person has when they have a mild physical pain but they are trying to bear through it. Or the look you get when the Chipotle employee is making your burrito and they are giving you visibly less meat than the burrito you saw them make before yours. It is a mixture between staying calm and internally wrestling emotionally. Terry was making this kind of face. As he spoke, he made it clear that he had not yet come around to my point of view on the subject we differed on, but that he had been thinking a lot about some of the points I made that were valid. In other words, he was "simultaneously holding two cognitions that were psychologically inconsistent"[5]. A belief that my points were valid, and a disagreement with my overall assessment. Terry was in a state of dissonance and that tension was showing up in his face. It was almost as if I could see his internal tension. What for me was even more interesting though, is that when I replied, I told him that I also thought he had made a really valid point. And when I made this statement I felt tension in my own forehead. I knew internally that I had not fully committed to his view either but that I was considering a point he made that was valid. I, like he, was in a state of dissonance and it was showing in my demeanor as well. The idea of having to simultaneously consider information that differed from my ideas and beliefs, while still holding on to my existing beliefs was causing me cognitive tension and discomfort. As Festinger stated, balancing differing cognitions is what leads to cognitive dissonance. This was Festinger's first observation.

Festinger's second key observation was birthed out of his first observation of cognitive dissonance in "The Seekers". Festinger noticed that as a result of their dissonance "The Seekers" remained in their dissonant state until they received the final message from their leader about Clarion. This message allowed "The Seekers" to have a sort of cognitive calming and sense of cognitive peace. Peace gained from having internal cognitive consistency. "The Seekers" no longer had to hold differing cognitions. The message from the leader provided a rationale for the differing cognitions that allowed them to no longer be contradictory, and this provided "The Seekers" with cognitive consistency. Festinger called this state of cognitive consistency, consonance. Festinger recognized that when an individual is in a dissonant state, internally they want to return to consonance. Cognitive dissonance is so strong that it produces an internal "drive" to relieve a person's cognitive discomfort.

Subsequent research on cognitive dissonance has found that to return back to consonance individuals will do four things. These things may be done individually or done in concert with each other. But when faced with dissonance, an individual may change their cognitions (beliefs, ideas, etc.), that is change their original ideas or beliefs to deal with the conflicting information. They may seek out more consonant information, which means they will look for more information that supports their view (this approach is called confirmation bias and will be discussed later in the chapter). They may trivialize the dissonant information by labeling it as flawed, discrediting the person delivering the information, downplaying how convincing the information is, or in other ways attempt to make the information not as impactful. Or they may avoid the dissonant information. Meaning that they find ways to avoid having to hear or engage with information that would lead to cognitive dissonance.

The last two options of trivializing dissonant information and avoiding dissonant information should feel somewhat familiar at this point. These are the two options that Gucci Mane illustrates in his verse when he says, "I'm not listening". Through his lyrics Gucci Mane provides an illustration of how the Hater Mindset trivializes and avoids dissonant information and by extension cognitive dissonance. Gucci Mane has made it clear by the name of the song that he believes the person giving him the information is a hater (dissenter), and thus should not be paid attention to. The information being provided has been trivialized by discrediting the person giving it. And because they are trivialized, Gucci Mane is "not listening". Meaning that he is avoiding the dissonant information. The first line of Gucci Mane's verse informs the listener that to handle his dissonance Gucci Mane has chosen a combination of trivialization and avoidance. He is "not listening". And by not listening he has found a way to avoid cognitive dissonance. This choice by Gucci Mane is representative of the choice of the Hater Mindset. Those who have embraced the Hater Mindset feel that hating or more accurately dissenting views cause them cognitive dissonance. And they choose to handle this dissonance by trivializing the dissenter and avoiding the dissent. By doing this, they have effectively eliminated dissonant information and by extension cognitive dissonance from their sphere. In other words, just like Gucci Mane they are "not listening"

"*So what if they're not listening".* These are the words I imagine any Hater Mindset supporter, and maybe even Gucci Mane himself might say at this point. In response to the discussion on cognitive dissonance they might reply:

> *"SO (dramatic pause) WHAT!! Simply explaining why people react to haters the way they do does not mean it is the wrong way. Or that they should change it.*

But doesn't it though?! You see, the Hater Mindset avoids cognitive dissonance by trivializing or avoiding dissonant information. And while this may protect individuals from discomfort and anxiety, cognitive dissonance has also been found to be a key part of positive experiences such as learning[6], civil dialogue and civility[7], and chiefly critical thinking[8].

Without cognitive dissonance there is, among other things, no critical thinking. And in the current fast paced ever-changing world critical thinking is vital. In fact, the concept of critical thinking has almost always been regarded as a positive part of human development. In the early 20th century there were writings heralding how there was a growing agreement that critical thinking was important and necessary for the future[9]. And today the importance of critical thinking is being emphasized in fields as diverse as nursing[10] to internet evaluation[11]. Almost every vocational field, government official, every educational level, and organizational leader is calling for increased critical thinking.

This is why the avoiding of cognitive dissonance is such a problem. Cognitive dissonance is a principal component of critical thinking. True critical thinking cannot occur without the genuine consideration and examination of dissonant information. In 2011, education scholar and endowed chair Steven Brookfield wrote a book titled *Teaching for Critical Thinking[12]*. In this text, Brookfield conceptualizes the idea of critical thinking in a simple four-step model. Step 1 is "hunting assumptions" often described as metacognition, or thinking about the way you are thinking. This is the intrapersonal process where we inwardly examine the assumptions that influence how we think and act. We look at *how* we are thinking (more on metacognition later). Step 2 is "checking assumptions". In this step, a critical thinker "tries to assess whether or not their assumptions are valid and reliable guides for action"[13]. They evaluate their own assumptions and thinking for errors or flaws. In a previous paper written on this topic I make the case that the Hater Mindset affects the successful completion of steps 1 and 2 of Brookfield's model. But in order to avoid diving into the depths of the effects of dissonant information on self-concepts and identity (identity and personality composition anyone?) I will focus here on the Hater Mindsets impact on the latter two steps of Brookfield's Model. Steps 3 and 4.

Step 3 of Brookfield's model is "seeing things

from different viewpoints". This step in the model calls for an individual to view the information they have in light of perspectives that differ from their own. To evaluate their own assumptions in light of ideas and information that are different. In essence, step 3 encompasses the idea of seeking out dissent and dissonant information. Therein lies the clash between critical thinking and the Hater Mindset. The Hater Mindset disdains and dismisses dissent because it can produce cognitive dissonance. However, critical thinking requires engagement with dissent. And a thorough engagement at that. In order for critical thinking to occur there must be consideration and engagement with differing ideas and cognitions. This engagement allows the ability to "see things from different viewpoints". Step 3 of Brookfield's model cannot be completed without information that is different from a person's existing cognitions; it requires dissonant information and cognitive dissonance. The Hater Mindset does the opposite of this; it avoids elements needed for critical thinking. And it prescribes this as the preferred way to handle cognitive dissonance. Thus leading to a culture that doesn't practice or value critical thinking. If any culture begins shifting toward avoiding dissent and trivializing dissenters as the preferred way to handle dissonant information and cognitive dissonance, that same culture is simultaneously shifting toward lower levels of critical thinking. A culture that values avoiding cognitive dissonance is one that is slowly losing its respect for and value of critical thinking. This is the effect of the Hater Mindset. It says, "I'm not listening" when dissent is around and thus it dampens the critical thinking capacity of those who embrace it.

Step 4 of Brookfield's Model is an outgrowth of step 3. Brookfield says step 4 in the critical thinking process is "taking informed action". Having identified their own assumptions, evaluated those assumptions for errors, and compared those assumptions to differing viewpoints and ideas, the critical thinker can move on to step 4 of "taking informed action". Informed action is grounded in information acquired through completing steps 1 through 3 in the critical thinking process. However, as pointed out, step 3 is in conflict with the Hater Mindset. An individual who has avoided dissonant information cannot take informed action. Specifically because they are not informed of any other perspectives other than their own. They avoided the information needed to evaluate their own assumptions. Thus because step 3 of critical thinking is hindered by the Hater Mindset, step 4 cannot occur either. So when Gucci Mane begins his verse "I'm not listening" what he is *really* saying is I'm dampening my critical thinking by avoiding dissent because it causes me cognitive dissonance. It's definitely not as catchy, but it may be far more accurate.

I'm Not Interested

"I'm not interested" is the second statement made by Gucci Mane in his vituperation against haters on the "haterade" song. In this lyric, Gucci Mane steps his Hater Mindset effects up a level, moving beyond "not listening" to point out that he is also "not interested". This lyric, like the last one, offers a new perspective on the effects of the Hater Mindset (who knew Gucci Mane was so deep). Here we learn that the Hater Mindset not only affects *access* to differing information by avoiding dissonant information, it also affects *interest*. And *interest* as it turns out is a vital component to learning. In fact, some scholars would argue that without interest there can be no genuine learning.

For an example of this consider the role interest played in a debate my friends and I were having once at a get together. We were not debating climate change, gun control, or any of the more controversial topics you may think of. We were debating something far closer to most people's heart. Something that truly impacts their lives. We were debating… who the best basketball player of all time was. Some of my friends and I, whose basketball fandom had come of age during the mid-90's, had firmly planted our feet on the unwavering and indisputable belief that Michael Jordan is the best basketball player ever. My supporting evidence included many of the standard propositions used to defend Michael Jordan as the best. Jordan never lost in the finals, he had two 3 peats, numerous scoring titles, finals M.V.P. multiple times, so on and so forth. The cohort of individuals who had taken their position in opposition to ours were advocating for LeBron James. They were not advocating for him to be called the best player of all time, but were proposing he should at least be in consideration (they told me when I wrote this, that it was important that I accurately portray their position. They have a reputation to protect). If you have attended a gathering of any kind that included passionate sport fans you have surely heard a similar discussion. The conversation was reaching its apex in volume when one of the members of the cohort in contention with mine said these words "yeah, Jordan never lost in the finals, but he didn't go 7 times in a row". I immediately paused, and two things happened next. I first turned to one of my friends who had aligned themselves with me and said, "how do you answer that?" My friend told me "don't trip, they just hating" and then continued on with the conversation. The next thing that happened is that I left the conversation, located the nearest smart phone, and spent the next 40 minutes looking up information related to LeBron James. His finals streak, stats, and more. After 40 minutes, I returned to the conversation (which was still going on. Yeah we are serious about our sports) with a revised view. I begin to tell my cohort that LeBron was the first person in 50 years to play in the number of finals games he has played in consecutively. I relayed what I had learned about his records and stats and his ability to add to various team stat "columns". Specifically I directed my comments about the finals to the friend who had told me they didn't care about the consecutive finals argument. I made sure to state that I had not converted my view but I did have a much better appreciation for LeBron and those who push for his consideration as the best basketball player in history. I distinctly remember that when I discussed the consecutive finals record and the 50 years context the friend who told me they didn't care about that argument indicated that they didn't know that information. As I was writing this book, I recognized that this statement by my friend represented a stark and important difference that had occurred between them and me during our greatest basketball player conversation. I had heard an argument from the opposing side that generated an information gap in me and I became interested, while my friend heard the same argument and was not interested. As a result, my interest caused me to seek out and learn quite a bit of information, that my friend did not know or learn that day. My interest was the difference between me learning and not learning something new. The fact that my friend who also heard the argument, was not interested, and instead chose to dub the arguments of the opposing side as hating, prevented them from learning.

In the story above, I referenced that the statement about LeBron James during the conversation generated an information gap that piqued my interest. The use of the term information gap was intentional. In psychology, an information gap is the uncomfortable feeling that arises when you sense that you don't know something that you are supposed to know. It's the feeling you get when you recognize a person's face but can't quite remember their name (next time try John or Sarah, it works). The term was coined the psychologist George Lowenstein in the early 1990's[14]. Lowenstein was interested in learning and used the term information gaps to describe the gaps between known information and unknown information. The gap represents the area in which you are interested or curious. One of the definitions of the word "interested" is to show curiosity about something. To be interested in something is to be curious about it. This is the point that author Ian Leslie makes in his book *Curious: The Desire to Know and Why Your Future Depends On It*[15] when discussing information gaps. For Leslie and Lowenstein, curiosity or interest is the fundamental aspect needed for learning. Lowenstein describes information gaps as cognitive itches on the brain. They spark a curiosity that must be scratched with new knowledge. This "scratching" is what leads to learning. The relief of the cognitive itching or information gap is achieved by learning the information you feel you should know. So information gaps actually lead directly to learning according to Lowenstein. Ian Leslie adds to the thoughts of Lowenstein by proposing that there are different types of information gaps.

> *There are known knowns. These are things we know that we know. There are known unknowns. That is to say, there are things that we know we don't know. But there are also unknown unknowns. There are things we don't know we don't know.*[16]

By comparing Lowenstein and Leslie's ideas with the second statement made by Gucci Mane in his Haterade verse, a better understanding of how the Hater Mindset hinders learning can be seen.

According to Lowenstein and Leslie information

gaps are created when individuals are introduced to ideas and information that differ from their own. This information produces doubt in an individual about what they know and this produces curiosity. Without this information people have what Leslie calls the "ignorant but happy effect". He writes, "when people are confident that they have the answers they become blithely incurious about alternatives"[17]. They are less interested and learn less. And as Eli Pariser points out in his book *The Filter Bubble: What the Internet is Hiding from You[18]*; people become over confident in their beliefs when all the information they are exposed to and interested in supports their view. Pariser argues this is what is happening in culture right now. "We've become overconfident in our beliefs and are learning less"[19]. However, when people are confronted with different ideas, information, and beliefs they are forced to question their own perspectives. This questioning generates interest and learning can occur.

The importance of different opinions and information to learning can be seen even more clearly when utilizing Leslie's different types of information gaps. Leslie lays out three categories of information gaps: known-knowns, known-unknowns, and unknown-unknowns. Two of these three categories of information gaps are fundamentally linked to interest in different perspectives. If in an individual has a known-unknown information gap, or information they know they don't know, they must naturally have been exposed to an area of information with which they are not familiar. Something that is different from their existing cognitive stores. This lets them know there is information out there that they don't know. If this information was indeed familiar it would simply be a known-known, but the fact that it represents a gap between what they know and some new information points to the information being from a perspective different from the one the individual currently holds. In other words, you have to hear about a different perspective for you to have a known-unknown. Similarly, if an individual has an unknown-unknown information gap, they cannot even identify this gap without being exposed to information that is distinct and different from their own. In order for someone to become aware of unknown-unknowns, they must have been exposed to information, perspectives, opinions, or worldviews that were not like their own. Unknown-unknowns are completely outside of an individual's cognitive reach without exposure to a different set of information or ideas. You can't know what you don't know if no one introduces you to that information. That information would forever exist as an unknown-unknown without this exposure. This brings us back to interest. In order to turn all of these information gaps into functional learning there must be one key component, interest.

This is why the Hater Mindset is so dangerous for learning. It diminishes interest. Gucci Mane's lyric "I'm not interested" illustrates that not only does the Hater Mindset not listen to different ideas, information, and beliefs; even if it does hear them, it is still not interested. Differing opinions, ideas, and beliefs do not generate information gaps for those enveloped in the Hater Mindset. Those who have fallen prey to the Hater Mindset respond to new perspectives, ideas, etc. that differ from their own in the same way that Gucci Mane does in the second line of his Haterade verse, "I'm not interested". Thus, they live in a perpetual state of the "ignorant but happy effect". They do not engage with their known-unknowns and they remain incessantly unaware and unable to access their unknown-unknowns. The Hater Mindset only has interest in its own information, conceptions, and ideas. And it uses these existing cognitions to construct a view of reality. The worldview of the Hater Mindset is constructed from the familiar and as Eli Pariser once wrote "a world constructed from the familiar is a world in which there's nothing to learn"[20].

My Attention Only Focused On What I Get

In the third line of Gucci Mane's treatise on the opinions of haters in the Haterade song he turns his focus to "attention". "My Attention Only Focused on What I Get" writes Gucci Mane. This third statement about attention in the midst of his discussion of haters seems odd. It's odd not only because it is grammatically incorrect (Gucci Mane certainly didn't consult his APA manual when he wrote that lyric) but odd in that "*attention*" in this context is starkly different from both "listening" and "interest". While listening and interest are processes that require little to no effort, *attention* on the other hand, cannot be divorced from effort. Merriam-Webster dictionary defines attention as *the act or state of applying the mind to something*[21]. Attention consists of both *an act*, "the act or state of". And of *application*, "applying the mind to something". Both action and application require effort. To act, you must expend effort in some way, and to apply anything to something else also requires effort. So when Gucci Mane says that his attention is only focused on what he gets, he actually reveals information about his internal cognitive effort. In truth, Gucci Mane actually reveals two distinct bits of information about his cognitive effort in this lyric. He reveals both where he is willing to expend cognitive effort, and where he is not willing to expend cognitive effort. And by doing so, he once again provides an example of how the Hater Mindset functions and offers insight on the impact of the Hater Mindset on contemporary culture. The Hater Mindset selectively applies cognitive effort. It has select areas where it will

102

and won't apply cognitive effort. And by selecting the areas that it has selected the Hater Mindset lowers epistemic motivation and strengthens confirmation bias.

Now before I proceed any further I can already imagine some readers saying, "It lowers epi... what? Did he just cuss at me?" No, I said it lowers epistemic motivation. In psychology epistemic motivation represents how likely you are to want to *really* understand something. It is defined as the "willingness to expend effort to achieve a thorough, rich, and accurate understanding of the world, including the group task or decision problem at hand"[22]. The effort referenced here is cognitive effort, or effort of the mind. It is effort that is aimed at making sure you have a better understanding of whatever information or situation is in front of you. Psychologist have found that epistemic motivation levels vary by individual and by situation. In terms of situation, certain people are more likely to seek out additional information in certain situations. For me, unique words send my epistemic motivation level through the roof. I love new words and when I hear one I can't wait to look it up and find out what it means. Words like "absquatulate" (which means to leave somewhere abruptly by the way) motivate me to apply cognitive effort to understand the situation in front of me. My epistemic motivation level for situations with unique words is most likely higher than other people's. However, while psychologists have seen that situations affect people's epistemic motivation, they have also shown that epistemic motivation is grounded in individual personality as well. In 2009, two scholars studying epistemic motivation made this point. They wrote

> Numerous studies indicate that individuals may either process information in a quick effortless, and heuristic way or do so in a more effortful,

103

deliberate, and systematic manner. Whether individuals engage in such systematic and thorough information processing depends on their **epistemic motivation**.[23]

The authors point, is that aspects of epistemic motivation are not based on situation but are based on personal characteristics specific to the individual. This means that some people have higher levels of epistemic motivation than others have in general, and are more likely to want to *really* understand situations more often than others are.

As an example, imagine if I were to tell a room full of people that there was a reptile in South America that eats flies. This statement would most likely cause different levels of epistemic motivation to occur. At the conclusion of my statement there would be several different reactions by my audience. Some of them would simply be content with my statement and would continue to listen. Unfazed by the flies and uninterested in the reptile. Others in the room would be filled with a copious amount of questions. What type of reptile? Where in South America? Does he know that is a whole continent? What type of flies? How big is the reptile? And any other number of questions filling their brain selected from the inexhaustible number of possible options available. However, these individuals, despite their abundance of curiosity will not seek out the answers to their questions. They won't deem it necessary to apply the cognitive effort to do so. They may be curious, but not enough to seek the answers. Still, there will be others in the group who will generate the same questions as those above, and will flock to the library, internet, smart phone, or whatever is available to find the answers to those questions. They will apply the cognitive effort needed to get the information because their epistemic motivation was higher. Whether that is because they love lizards, like to learn, or just like to see if people are lying to them, they are willing to expend the cognitive effort necessary to obtain the answers. They intrinsically have higher levels of epistemic motivation.

However, the intrinsic nature of epistemic motivation is not the only significant observation scholars have made about the concept. In addition to recognizing that it is tied to individual characteristics, psychologists also learned that epistemic motivation is malleable. That unlike IQ or other mental capacities that are more or less fixed, epistemic motivation can be increased or decreased. This malleability is what is relevant for the Hater Mindset. The approach of the Hater Mindset toward cognitive effort is one that decreases epistemic motivation while increasing confirmation bias.

In Gucci Mane's third line we learn that his "attention only focused on what he gets" (again with the bad grammar, come on Gucci). In this statement, Gucci Mane not only tells us where he is willing to apply his cognitive effort, or better yet, where he has high levels of epistemic motivation. He also tells us where he is not putting that cognitive effort or where his epistemic motivation is low. And he is not willing to put his cognitive effort in anything outside of "what he gets". "What he gets" of course being his opinion, interests, and bias. In other words, Gucci Mane is stating that he is only willing to apply cognitive effort to understand those things that he already knows and agrees with. He is practicing confirmation bias. Confirmation Bias in psychology is essentially the opposite of epistemic motivation. It is the tendency to search for, interpret, favor, and recall information in a way that confirms one's preexisting beliefs or hypotheses. As mentioned earlier confirmation bias responds to cognitive dissonance by seeking more consonant information. It is not concerned with obtaining a thorough, rich, and accurate understanding, instead it is focused on showing rightness. "My rightness" to be exact. Not "my" as in me Wes Parham, but "my" as in whoever is utilizing this bias. Confirmation bias is often called "myside bias". The individual who practices confirmation bias is able to ignore all information that counters "their side", while confidently asserting information that confirms their view. Hence "myside bias". You have probably seen or been this person in an argument. During the argument with this person, every bit of conflicting information is disregarded, while every confirming bit of information is given the weight of the world. The person doing this is practicing confirmation bias, and a hallmark of confirmation bias is that a person applies more cognitive effort toward information that confirms their views than they do any other information.

The issue of course with confirmation bias, is that it leads to more confirmation bias, and eventually produces declines in epistemic motivation. As Schulz points out in her book *Being Wrong: Adventures in the Margin of Error*[24], when we only engage with information that supports our view we become overconfident and certain of our own rightness. This certainty about our rightness makes us less likely to search for other information or seek a thorough understanding, because we believe we already have it. Thus, our epistemic motivation begins to decline. Why be willing to put forth effort to obtain a thorough, rich, and accurate understanding of something if you already have one, right? And if the information that gains your attention confirms your existing views as right, then you can be confident about most things, and have no reason to have higher levels of epistemic motivation in general. The problem with this approach is that both high amounts of confirmation bias and lower levels of epistemic motivation have been shown to have detrimental effects.

106

The research I conducted to complete my Ph.D. was on epistemic motivation. I wanted to know if higher levels of epistemic motivation made people more innovative. The American war college described today's geopolitical world as a V.U.C.A. world. That is Volatile Uncertain, Complex, and Ambiguous. This term has since seeped over into the organizational literature as a way to describe the world in general, and its advent has led to an emphasis on innovation. In order to succeed in today's world innovation is needed in almost every aspect of society. My research was on whether higher levels of epistemic motivation would produce the innovation needed to succeed in today's world. The findings showed that epistemic motivation is directly related to innovative behavior. People with higher levels of epistemic motivation are usually more innovative. However, that isn't all. These individuals also have higher levels of empathy, better decision making, higher levels of social capital and organizational trust, and higher levels of critical thinking. And these are just a few of the benefits associated with high epistemic motivation. Conversely, those with low epistemic motivation are harder to motivate, show less commitment and innovation, have weaker organizational relationships, and make worse decisions when faced with complicated problems.

In the same vein, confirmation bias has also been found to have strong correlations with positive behavior, but in reverse correlation. Individuals with low levels of confirmation bias were found to be more open-minded, more collaborative, able to better synthesize information, and even more resilient to perceived failure. Whereas psychologists chronicling high levels of confirmation bias, have found it leading to bad financial decisions, self-deceptions, bad medical decisions, weaker team decisions, and more. Schulz in her book *Being Wrong* makes the case that an adherence and overconfidence in the belief that we are right (a byproduct of confirmation bias) can serve as the foundation for tyranny, war, and any other number of negative elements.

Thus, any approach to knowledge and information that results in the combination of increasing confirmation bias and declining epistemic motivation has the potential for devastating effects. This is my fear with the Hater Mindset. The person or culture who has adopted the Hater Mindset, like Gucci Mane, chooses to place their cognitive effort on "what they get". By doing so they have accepted an approach to information that can only lead to an increase in confirmation bias and a decline in epistemic motivation. Which ultimately has negative effects for both individuals and the culture.

Summary

At the outset of this chapter I argued that the first three lines of Gucci Mane's verse on his haterade song introduces the outcomes that a dismissal and disdain for dissent have on individuals and their thinking. I made the argument that these three lines can serve as a treatise on the Hater Mindsets approach to dissent and dissenters. And these three lines outline how the Hater Mindset leads individuals to not listen, which makes them less likely to of be critical thinkers. It leads them to not be interested, which hinders their learning. And it causes them to only focus their attention on "what they get", which leads to lower levels of epistemic motivation and higher levels of confirmation bias. And while this chapter was designed to focus on the negative implications of what a dismissal and disdain for dissent inevitably produce, my hope is that at the same time the reverse happened. That at the same time that negative implications of disdaining and dismissing dissent were being shared, you as a reader were able to glean and extol the virtues of embracing dissent and its needed role in society. If the disdaining and dismissal of dissent produced by the Hater Mindset leads to lower levels of critical thinking, less learning, lower levels of epistemic motivation, and higher levels of confirmation bias, then embracing dissent should have the opposite effect. And so while the Hater Mindset says to disdain dissent, I challenge you to "Be a Hater" (more on this later) and embrace, seek out, and intentionally engage dissent. If the consequences of disdaining and dismissing dissent are so detrimental, the benefits of its engagement are probably equally as sweet.

PART 3 - "YOU"

Chapter 6 –I'm Projecting, That's Why You're The Problem!!

"No it's not me, it's not me, the problem is not me. It's you"
-Wes Parham (Spoken Word)

Before I began writing this book, but after I had already begun studying the Hater Mindset, I wrote a spoken word piece (a type of poem) to express my thoughts on the topic. At the time, I hadn't fully formulated my ideas to the degree that I have here, but wanted to find a way to get some of my preliminary thoughts out into the world. A spoken word piece seemed like a great way to do that. I structured the piece similarly to the way this book is laid out. With each section addressing a different part of the sentence, "You are just a hater". And although I think there are several great lines in the piece (I might be a little bias), the section that focuses on "You" I think really gets to the heart of the "You idea" in the "You are just a hater" sentence. Some of the quotes from the piece that I think encapsulate the "You" idea are (in no particular order):

> *"You see I have to call you a hater, because otherwise I have to look at me."*
> *"No it's not me, it's not me, the problem is not me. It's you!!"*
> *"In my mind it has to be you. It has to be you because if it is not you that means it's me."*
> *"If I see me inwardly, I might have to acknowledge the problem is not you, it's me."*

What I like about these lines is that they hint at a paradox that I believe occurs when someone calls someone else a hater. It is a paradox that I also hinted at in the first chapter of this book. It is the paradox of projection.

In chapter one, I asserted that when someone calls someone else a hater it actually shows that the *labeler,* the person calling someone a hater, has a disdain for dissent. My wording here was intentional. In stating it this way I intentionally attribute certain understandings and cognitions not to the labeled individual, the one called the hater; but to the labeler, the one doing the calling. This is the paradox of projection I believe exists in the "you are just a hater" sentence. And the one hinted at in my quotes above. The "You" in the sentence, while meant to draw attention to the labeled individual, instead reflects back on the labeler. It is a projection. In both psychological and organizational literature, the idea that an individual's actions or even their beliefs toward others can reveal information about themselves has been thoroughly studied. In fact, the idea that observing a person's behaviors toward others can reveal information about that person may be the most well known idea in the field of psychology, and even outside of it. While people who don't work in the field of mental health may not be familiar with terms like "the cycle of conflict" or "psychodynamic theory", they *are* usually familiar with the term "projection". It is not uncommon to hear an individual tell another in the midst of a heated debate, "you're projecting". What they are really saying is, "your behaviors right now are a reflection of you not me". This same idea of projection is found in organizational literature as well. In an article for Human Resource Management International Digest Ann Betz[1] wrote, "Our feedback to someone often reveals more about ourselves than it does about the other person". Betz's statement echoes the concept of projection and at the same time rings true for our discussion of the word "You". Betz

114

statement specifically references the feedback that we give to other individuals, and says that this feedback actually reveals more about ourselves than the other person. And what is labeling another person a hater if not feedback. Feedback on the person's thoughts, behaviors, actions, or whatever other information was shared. That feedback actually allows more to be learned about the person saying it than the person it is being said to. This is the paradox of projection in the "You" part of the "You are just a hater" sentence. By calling someone a hater "you" actually reveal more about yourself.

However, this isn't the whole story. The allure of the concept of projection isn't just that you can find out information about the person speaking, the allure is *what* you can find out about the person speaking. Since its establishment as a term and concept, projection has been recognized as a psychological defense mechanism. A way for humans to defend themselves against subconscious thoughts, fears, ideas, qualities, or other cognitive elements they find unacceptable in themselves by attributing them to others. This is what makes projection interesting. Through examining a person's projections it is possible to get a glimpse of what someone may subconsciously fear. There are two points in this conception of projection that are important for our discussion, defense and subconscious.

The idea of defense is an interesting one because it assumes harm or danger. Typically, when people feel the need to defend themselves, it is in response to the possibility of harm or an expectation of danger. Projection was identified as a way that people respond to these possibilities. The immediate question is, harm from who and danger from what? Psychologists would say that projection is the individual's way of protecting themselves from harm to their self-image and the danger that their self-image is incorrect. People naturally form an image of how they believe themselves to be and this image becomes central to their identity. A danger to that image is essentially a danger to the people themselves. Thus, people will, and do, go to great lengths to protect their self-image. In the case of projection, people have a subconscious idea that something is disrupting their self-image. This disruption represents a challenge to the individual's self-image that they can't accept. So instead of accepting that their self-image is wrong, the individual projects this subconscious disruption onto someone else.

So how does this relate to the Hater Mindset and the idea of the "You"? I maintain that the "You" in the "You are just a hater" sentence represents a projection. The person who says this statement is actually projecting a subconscious fear on to someone else. Based on the discussion above however, in order for this to be true, the person calling someone a hater would have to be defending themselves from something that they believe would distort their self-image, and is also subconsciously unacceptable. The logical question is what could this thing be? What idea could be so universally dangerous that anyone who feels the need to call someone a hater could be projecting? I have argued to this point that the Hater Mindset is globally pervasive. And with it being globally pervasive all kinds of different people, have fallen prey to it. People from different ethnicities, ages, backgrounds, socioeconomic levels, and more. With so unique a group of people and such a wide range of self-images, what idea could they all view as subconsciously so dangerous that they feel the need to project onto someone else? The answer to this question is a simple one, but one that has profound implications. The idea that is seen as universally dangerous to self-images is the idea of wrongness. The dangerous idea that is subconsciously feared, and thus projected, is the potential that they are wrong.

116

In 2010, Kathryn Schulz published what I consider one of the greatest books I've read in the last 50 years. Granted I'm not 50 years old yet, but her text still remains one of the most engaging and insightful I have had the pleasure of reading. The book titled *Being Wrong: Adventures in the Margin of Error* is described as "an illuminating exploration of what it means to be in error, and why homo sapiens tend to tacitly assume (or loudly insist) that they are right about most everything"[2]. In the first chapter of Schulz book she makes two points that are relevant to the discussion of projection. She first states that as human beings we love to be right and we hate to be wrong. To be more precise we revel in the idea of being right. And about being right about anything. As humans, we find pleasure in being right indiscriminate of subject. Politics, sports, food, movies, where the TV remote is, where we left our cellphones, all subjects that we are delighted to find out we were right about. Schulz argues this is part of human nature. And because we delight in being right we believe, as Schulz says that we are "basically right, basically all the time, about basically everything"[3]. This belief in our rightness plays a distinct role in our self-image. It allows us to view ourselves as capable, intelligent, and trustworthy. If we are right, we are capable, we are smart, we can be trusted. On the reverse side, people hate to be wrong. To be wrong challenges our self-image. It makes us doubt those things that we so confidently believed ourselves to be. Maybe we are not smart, capable, or trustworthy. And since being wrong does this to our self-image we rarely ever believe ourselves to be wrong. Schulz writes that people tend to view being wrong as an aberration. Something that is rare and bizarre. Thus when faced with the possibility that we are wrong, we find its presence unacceptable in ourselves. Which is of course the first prerequisite for projection.

However, if Schulz is correct this creates quite a

quandary. As beings with the capacity for rationality, we must recognize the potential for wrongness. We cannot honestly believe ourselves to be omniscient, so we know that there are areas where we must be wrong. And as such, these areas are potentially threats to our self-image. The problem is that we are not consciously aware of these areas, and cannot be consciously aware of them. If I were to ask you if all of your beliefs are correct, you would probably answer no. However, if I was to say which one of your beliefs are wrong, you would most likely be unable to answer. If you believe something, you believe it to be true. So if you believed it to be wrong, you would stop believing it. Schulz calls this concept error blindness. We are always blind to our current errors. This is the quandary. We know that we are not 100% right, but we never know where we are wrong. As such, we live in a perpetual state of confidence and doubt. Confidence about our beliefs, but doubt that they are 100% correct. And as long as we only interact with our own thoughts and opinions the potential for wrongness remains latent, almost abstract. It exists in an ethereal sense, but not as a threat to our self-image. Because it is real, but not present. The problem comes when we are exposed to the thoughts and opinions of others, that are different than are own. It is at this point that the subconscious mind becomes aware of the threat of wrongness. A threat that has implications for a person's self-image. This of course is the second prerequisite for projection. A subconscious threat to self-image.

Recognizing that wrongness is a threat to self-image, but one that occurs at the subconscious level, it makes sense how the fear of wrongness leads to projection. The self-image of an individual is unwilling to consider wrongness in themselves, and subconsciously wrongness is a threat to that individual's self-image. Thus when faced with the potential that they are wrong, a

118

person may project that wrongness. This is what I am proposing happens with the "You" in the statement "You are just a hater". The "you" here represents a projection of wrongness. This is clearly what is implied when someone makes the statement "You are just a hater". What they are saying is you are wrong. You are asserting wrong ideas. Rather than accept that they themselves may be wrong, the person who says, "you are just a hater" projects this possible wrongness onto the other person. Thereby absolving themselves of any possibility of being wrong and preserving their self-image. And I contend that the Hater Mindset makes this a practice. Those infected with the Hater Mindset will consistently react to differing information and perspectives with projection. And it is this action that I believe leads to the second major negative outcome of the Hater Mindset. Entitlement.

Why you so entitled?

Entitlement is a loaded term in today's society. Most people associate it with government programs, the poor, the rich, democrats, republicans, or some other politically and controversially charged term. In truth, entitlement is defined in the dictionary as the belief that one is inherently deserving of the right to something[4]. It is the idea that someone has an undisputable and uncontested right to something. And for me it is the natural outcome of projecting wrongness.

In some cases entitlement is a good thing. The Declaration of Independence states:

> "We hold these truths to be self-evident, that all men are created equal, that they are endowed by their Creator with certain unalienable Rights"

This statement seems to imply that all men are entitled to

inalienable rights. They are undisputed and cannot be questioned. This I would argue is a good thing; we have seen what happens when individuals are not entitled to these rights. The rights are trampled on, as we saw with chattel slavery for over 400 years. So in this case, entitlement to inalienable rights is a good thing. But what happens when entitlement moves into the realm of individual cognition? Which is what will inevitably happen when a person never has to confront the idea that their thoughts are wrong. Projection and entitlement are linked together. Bowling Green State psychology professor Joshua Grubbs argues that entitled people tend to direct their anger outward (project), choosing to blame others while self-confirming their own uniqueness[5]. If each time a person is faced with the possibility that their cognitions are wrong, they are able to reject that idea by projecting that fear of wrongness onto someone else, eventually they will not feel a need to question their ideas at all. They will assume that they have a right to them, because they are right. And they are right because they believe them. It creates an ironclad (at least in the mind of the person who holds this belief) circle of logic that need not be questioned or evaluated. It actually creates an entitlement (the belief that one is inherently deserving of the right to something) to "entitlements".

That last sentence can be confusing if you are not an epistemologist or at least somewhat familiar with the study of epistemology. Epistemology is the study of the theory of knowledge. How do people know what they know? What is knowledge? Can you know it and how can you know it? These are just some of the questions epistemologists investigate. In epistemology there is a type of belief called an "entitlement". The epistemologist Tyler Burge defines an entitlement as "a form of justification of one's beliefs where reasons do not need to be made explicit"[6]. In other words, it is a belief a person feels they have a warrant to hold without any explicit justification for that warrant. An idea held with no supporting justification for it being held. This type of "entitlement" has been used to explain why children have a right to the ideas that they do. According to "entitlement" advocates, children should not have to provide rational justifications for their beliefs in order for them to have the right to hold them. They may have picked up their justifications subconsciously and not be able to explain them, they may have gotten them from an authority they trust, or any other number of reasons. And so, the child may have the right to hold their beliefs even if they can't justify why they hold them. And although this type of belief has been attributed to children, I argue that "entitlements" become a regular staple in the mind of those who have fallen prey to the Hater Mindset. The person who never has to consider the idea that their beliefs may be wrong will begin to create a self-imposed impregnable border around their ideas. They will feel they are right to hold their beliefs because those beliefs are right. And since they do not perceive themselves as wrong, their ideas need not be justified. So in essence the individual will believe they have an uncontested right to hold ideas and beliefs that have no justification. They become entitled to entitlements.

As an example consider a recent situation that occurred and attracted a lot of attention in the media. A philosophy professor at a liberal arts college was instructed by the Dean of his school to remove the philosophy of religion portion of the class from his intro to philosophy course. Apparently, a student in the class, who described himself as religious was offended by the presentation of arguments against God being taught in the class. In this student's mind these arguments represented an attack on his faith. It is important to note that the philosophy of religion has a long history that includes philosophers on both sides of the existence of God. While the field includes notable atheist philosophers such as Albert Camus, Sam Harris, Daniel Dennett, and more. The field is also equally filled with theistic scholars like Augustine, Thomas Aquinas, William Lane Craig and others. What is interesting about this whole situation is the student didn't argue that he was not provided adequate time to respond or present his justification for believing in God. Or even that equal weight was not given to the arguments for God. In fact, no reference to a defense or justification for his beliefs was reported at all. Instead, he simply felt that he had a right to his beliefs and so he was not the problem. The professor was. The student's entitlement to his beliefs caused him to believe "the real problem" was the professor not himself. Thus, he had no reason to examine or even justify his belief. Instead, he projected the problem onto the teacher, and asked the Dean to intervene.

At the core of the "You" in the "you are just a hater sentence" is the idea of projection. The person who has fallen prey to the Hater Mindset will avoid the possibility that they themselves are wrong. They will instead project their fear of being wrong on to someone else. This projection creates a situation where that individual can now feel that they are entitled to their beliefs. They will feel entitled to those beliefs, because all wrongness happens around them, but not to them. As Schulz says they will think that they are "basically right, basically all the time, about basically everything." And whenever the thought that they may be wrong creeps in they will respond like the quotes that I mentioned earlier in the chapter.

"No it's not me, it's not me, the problem is not me. It's you!!"

122

Chapter 7 – You Can't Tell Me Nothing... I'm Supergirl

"You did what you thought was right and no one could blame you for that."
- Martian Manhunter on Supergirl

In all honesty as I first thought about the role of the "you" in the "you are just a hater" sentence, I didn't initially see why it was a problem. As I thought about the concept I was immediately able to see that it was a projection. A way to shift focus from oneself to another person. And I could see how this projection naturally gave individuals an entitlement approach to their thoughts and opinions. What I didn't initially see is why this entitlement made me uncomfortable. Why it is actually a problem. Why is entitlement and the entitlement to entitlements something that we as individuals and the greater culture should be concerned about? Media, bloggers, teachers, and even researchers talk at great length about entitlement usually with the perspective that is has negative consequences. But as I thought about the concept, I struggled to answer the question "so what". I'm not talking about physical entitlement, or entitlement programs, which often are the source of great debate. I'm talking about cognitive entitlement. What is really so bad about people feeling like they are entitled to their thoughts and beliefs, without a justification? It wasn't until early in 2017, while watching an episode of Supergirl, that my thoughts on cognitive entitlement began to change. The ideas espoused in Supergirl that day illuminated for me the dangers of cognitive entitlement and its infusion into culture.

I would love to tell you that I had some ultra-noble reasons for watching Supergirl. That I was watching because I have daughters and wanted them to see a strong female lead, or because I am a complementarian feminist and wanted to help boost ratings for a show featuring an empowered woman. The truth however is much deeper. Deep down at the core of my being, in the most inner depths of my personality I … am a superhero. At least I pretended I was during most of my childhood. I grew up in the comic book era and have been enamored with the idea of heroes and villains, cosmic and super alike ever since. This fascination with all things Superhero remained unfettered up until DC made Batman vs Superman and showed me that it is possible to make a Superhero movie that I won't enjoy (you broke my heart Batman vs Superman). On this particular day however, I was watching a Supergirl episode simply titled "Alex". The TVline.com description of the episode was "As Alex fights for her life, Kara and Maggie team up for a rescue". The episode centered around Supergirl's adopted sister Alex, and Supergirl's attempt to save her. For brevity sake I will not include a full description of the episode here, but I will briefly describe the scenes that caught my attention. These three scenes illustrated the three natural, and I would argue dangerous, effects that derive from cognitive entitlement and pose a danger to the current culture. Those effects being a decline in the practice of metacognition, the development of guiltlessness, and chronic disappointment.

Declining Metacognition

"Then what *is* the right question?" These were the words spoken in frustration by Supergirl in the first scene that caught my attention. At this point, Supergirl and her team have recognized that Alex is in danger and are trying to figure out how to track down the perpetrators. The team is discussing the lack of evidence surrounding Alex's situation when one of the team members says, "we're asking the wrong question". Supergirl, obviously frustrated, responds with the words "Then what *is* the right question?" This is actually not an unusual response, especially in TV. It is actually an expected one. In TV land when someone says, "you're asking the wrong question" you are obligated to either ask the right question or respond by saying "what *is* the right question". The goal of this exchange is to get the characters present to think differently about the situation. Questions allow people to use a different paradigm with which to view a given challenge. One of my favorite examples of this is in the movie the Matrix. There is a scene in the movie where Morpheus and Neo are fighting and Neo is losing. Morpheus walks over to Neo and asks, "Do you believe that my being stronger or faster has anything to do with my muscles in this place?" He then pauses and leans over Neo, who is gasping for air, and says, "Do you think that's air you're breathing now?" The goal of Morpheus' questions were to get Neo to think differently about his situation. To change his perspective, to shift his paradigm. In the end this is exactly what happened. Neo, once again fights Morpheus but this time he is able to move at superhuman speed while doing so. The questions asked to him allowed him to tap into different cognitive skills than he was previously using. What caught my attention about Supergirl's version of the "what *is* the right question" response was how exasperated she appeared to be. In many of the cases where you see this exchange occur, the person who says, "what is the right question" is usually depicted as more curious than frustrated. The characters typically recognize that the point of saying "we are asking the wrong question" is to get them to tap into their cognitive stores for a different set of skills. Supergirl's response curiously was not curiosity but frustration. She was depicted as being at her wit's end. The question didn't cause a paradigm shift for Supergirl, just additional exasperation.

The second scene that caught my attention was a conversation between Supergirl and Alex's girlfriend, Maggie. In this scene, the team helping Supergirl believes they have made a breakthrough in finding Alex. As a result Supergirl runs (flew is probably more accurate) off without thoroughly assessing the situation and ends up making the situation worse. However, the conversation that happens before she does this caught my eye. Before Supergirl went off to make her mistake, Maggie warned Supergirl that her standard approach of punch first and think later would not work in this situation. Maggie ardently argued that this situation required a different type of thinking. She provides several evidence based reasons for her conclusion. Supergirl, feeling entitled to her approach and unable to consider the possibility of being wrong (this was discussed in chapter 5), responded by utilizing the same approach she was used to. And the same one she had just been warned would not work based on the evidence. She flew off attempted to use force to solve the situation, and ended up making the situation worse. What stood out to me in the conversation between Maggie and Supergirl was Maggie's identification of Supergirl's approach to problem solving. Maggie tells Supergirl that she can't punch her way out of this problem. By doing so, she identifies the fact that Supergirl has a preferred way of dealing with problem solving. Supergirl tries to solve problems with force.

The combination of these two scenes shed light on one of the natural outcomes of cognitive entitlement. They illustrate how Supergirl's cognitive entitlement caused her to rely on a heuristic based decision approach for solving problems. Because of her cognitive entitlement, as demonstrated by the conversation with Maggie (and in the third scene that caught my attention, to be discussed later), she did not and could not utilize metacognition to adjust her thinking. This is a natural outcome of cognitive entitlement. It leads to an over reliance on heuristic based decisions.

I do recognize that in making this assertion I introduced two terms that many people might not be familiar with, heuristic and metacognition. So allow me to clarify these terms. A heuristic is essentially a mental shortcut. It is a strategy for solving problems and making judgements when information is limited, that is derived from previous knowledge and experiences. Whenever a problem or situation occurs your brain has a massive amount of information and strategies it can use to solve the problem. Take for instance you getting hot. When you get hot there are any number of things you can do. You could build a shade shed out of the nearest tree. You could fan yourself with your hands. You could spit on your arms and blow your breath on the spit to get a cool feeling (that's gross but it's an option). You can jump fully clothed into the nearest body of water. You can lay in the grass assuming it is cooler. Any of these options may work to cool you off. Heuristics rely on previous knowledge and experience, and are designed to help with the quick resolution of routine and unambiguous tasks[1]. Which is why when you get hot you don't go through the massive number of choices possible to cool yourself off. Instead, you simply look for a cold glass of water to drink. Your brain, based on past experiences, created a mental shortcut or heuristic to solve the problem. "If I'm getting hot, I will get a glass of water." In this way, heuristics are quite beneficial and needed. They simplify routine tasks and problems so that we can survive and function efficiently. However, an over reliance on heuristic thinking can cause us to make suboptimal decisions, and even prevent us from seeing other alternatives to solving problems. As an example, take our water drinking heuristic. A heuristic of drinking water to cool off could be dangerous in an area where the water is contaminated, polluted, or infected with poisonous insects. This heuristic in that area would lead to a suboptimal decision. Similarly, the heuristic of drinking a cup of water to cool down is useless in an uninhabited desert. In this case, the focus on getting a glass of water could prevent an individual from finding other possible options available to them. Their heuristic thinking would impair a person's ability to use their metacognition to discover other alternatives.

Metacognition is of course the act of thinking about thinking and being able to monitor and control one's own cognitions[2]. Metacognition is not about *what* you are thinking but moreso *how* you are thinking. A more thorough understanding can be drawn from the work of French researcher Joelle Proust. Proust identifies what she calls a mental action. A mental action is when a mental process, strategy, idea, or event is called on and made available to the brain's executive process in order to accomplish a mental goal[3]. Proust parallels it to the physical action of turning on a light in a room. The physical act of turning on the light was completed because of the goal of needing to see. In the same way when the brain recognizes a goal it calls upon certain cognitive processes and makes them available to executive processes of the brain. Metacognition is focused on this process. It looks at what cognitive strategies and events are called on and how and when they are made available to executive processes[4]. It evaluates the mental processes that are occurring, and controls which one's are used. It asks why do I value this? Why do I think like that? How did I come to this decision? Or the question every parent asks while changing yet another outfit their child spilled their breakfast on (I keep forgetting to let them eat before getting them dressed). It's the same one I ask whenever I go to the Chipotle where I know they give small portions. "Why do I keep doing this?" And after asking these questions, it controls the thinking process to make it more optimal. Metacognition, like heuristic thinking, is a necessary part of cognitive processes. It has been linked to emotional coping (why am I sad) and to personal growth (how do I not make this same mistake next time). In educational psychology it has been shown to improve oral and written communication and increase the speed and accuracy of analysis of complex situations related to the human experience. But for the purposes of our discussion, it is important to know that it has been linked to changing and evaluating which mental strategies are used for a given situation. Metacognition is what allows us to catch the flaws in our heuristic and other thinking and correct them.

This concept of metacognition being used to revise the flaws in our thinking process was demonstrated in a study described by Harvard trained brain and mind expert Maya Bialik[5]. Bialik described research on metacognition that involved studying the difference between seasoned mathematicians and students. Bialik wrote

> "students were compared to seasoned mathematicians. The students consistently selected a seemingly useful strategy (heuristic) and continued to apply it without checking to see if it was actually working. They wasted a significant amount of time on fruitless pursuits. The more experienced mathematicians on the other hand, exercised metacognition, monitoring their approach all along the way to see if it was

129

actually leading to a solution or a dead end. Rather than just using what they had learned, they thought about how they were using what they had learned – and that made a huge difference."

The mathematician's metacognition along the way made a significant difference in their thinking process, not just in the way they answered questions. This is one of the benefits of metacognition. It allows an individual to monitor and control their thinking process and strategies. It allows an individual to choose to think differently. It is metacognition that allowed Neo to be able to defeat Morpheus. And it was the lack of metacognition which led Supergirl to be frustrated when asking "what *is* the right question". Her failure to use her metacognition was what caused her to be unable to see the need for a different approach when confronted by Maggie and before flying off to worsen the situation.

As I stated before Supergirl could not and did not use metacognition to adjust her thinking because it was impaired by her cognitive entitlement. Supergirl's cognitive entitlement was demonstrated through her response to Maggie's conversation with her about Supergirl's punch first ask questions later approach. When Maggie confronts Supergirl about rushing off, Maggie lays out several facts to support and explain her position. She essentially offers a cognitive justification to Supergirl on why Supergirl's current beliefs were incorrect. In response to Maggie's argument and evidence, Supergirl does not offer a justification for her position. She does not even explain why Maggie's position is wrong. She simply says, "I'm going" and flies off. This is the very definition of cognitive entitlement discussed in the previous chapter. To believe your approach is right without any justification for believing so. In fact, Supergirl's actions seem odd if cognitive entitlement *is not* at play. If someone offers a justification and rationale for a course of action, this usually warrants a response. Especially in serious situations. Imagine if this was the case in a presidential debate. Since the president of the United States is such an important position, a justification or a defense of statements is expected. If one candidate were to get up and say to their opponent, "your approach to leading this country will lead us into turmoil and despair. It is the wrong approach." And the other candidate was to respond, "I'm doing it my way", this would be a bizarre response by any stretch of the imagination. Yet, in a life and death situation for her sister, this is exactly Supergirl's response. Supergirl felt entitled to her belief that she had the right approach. She did not need a justification or a defense. Her approach was the right one because she believed it to be.

This cognitive entitlement by Supergirl caused her to get stuck in heuristic thinking. Remember heuristic thinking creates a mental shortcut and preferred way of handling problems. It can prevent people from seeing other approaches to solving problems. In the case of Supergirl, Supergirl was frustrated throughout the episode because the heuristic she was using was not effective at solving this particular problem. At one point Supergirl had no evidence, no suspect, and no direction. She wanted to use her heuristic of "force first, questions later" to solve the problem but had no one to direct the force toward. Thus, she becomes frustrated when someone says she is asking the wrong questions. She is frustrated because she could not think out of her preferred heuristic and so questions that challenged her to do so only bred exasperation. To be clear Supergirl had plenty of other cognitive resources she could have relied on. Throughout the series she has shown herself to be extremely intelligent. However, in situations with her sister, Supergirl had always used force, and reliance on this force

131

heuristic prevented her from accessing her other cognitive processes. She could not even see them. Her entitlement was preventing her metacognition. She was essentially looking for a glass of water in an uninhabited desert.

Supergirl's behavior in the two scenes outlined above illustrate the first natural outcome of cognitive entitlement, and are representative of what occurs in those who have the Hater Mindset. A decline in metacognition. Those who feel cognitively entitled are less likely to evaluate their cognitions and the processes that developed them. Thus, they will have lower levels of metacognition, and are more likely to get "stuck" in heuristic thinking. This assertion is supported by several studies in educational scholarship, psychological literature, legal literature, and organizational theory, which have reported lower levels of self -awareness and self-efficacy (variables that have been shown to be related to metacognition) as well as lower levels of metacognition itself in Generation Z and Millennials. As an example, J. Palmer writing in the Cleveland Law Review wrote that when what Millennials expect to happen, or feel entitled to happen, does not happen it can leave them feeling lost with a lack of direction[6]. Just like Supergirl when the established heuristic doesn't work, Millennials often feel lost or frustrated. They cannot adjust, think about where their thinking was incorrect and correct it. In many cases, Palmer writes that they may just abandon the effort altogether. And with no effort they inadvertently limit access to the cognitive resources available to them and rely on existing strategies for solving problems. They rely on heuristics and stifle their innovative and novel approaches to problem solving.

As an organizational scholar, this result is scary. Today's organizations function in a VUCA (Volatile, Uncertain, Complex, Ambiguous) environment[7]. VUCA environments require individuals who are willing and able to bring novel ideas to problems. Individuals that don't rely on heuristic based thinking. VUCA environments require innovation. And locking onto any heuristic based thinking in a way that inhibits the examination of alternatives is going to limit an individual's capacity for innovation. The scholars Korhonen and team write, "to succeed in the current business environment, organizations need to be innovative... in the face of uncertainty, complexity and change"[8]. And since "it is, ultimately, individuals who generate ideas and are responsible for turning those ideas into a reality"[9] organizations need individuals who are able to use their metacognition to control and monitor their thinking process and who are able to think outside of existing heuristics. This is where the Hater Mindset is dangerous. It creates cognitive entitlement which leads to an over-reliance on heuristic based thinking and a decline in meta-cognition. Which ultimately impacts thinking, innovation, and more.

Guiltless Ethics

The third scene that caught my attention in the Supergirl "Alex" episode points to another danger of cognitive entitlement and the Hater Mindset. Those in the Hater Mindset are encouraged to be guiltless. The scene that demonstrated this point was the conversation Supergirl had with her friend and sage advisor, Hank Henshaw (or the Martian Manhunter, depending on what form he is in). After Supergirl returns from worsening the situation by rushing in too hastily, she finds an isolated place to sulk. It is here that she is approached by Hank Henshaw. During their conversation the following dialogue takes place.

> *Supergirl: Maggie was right, I shouldn't have rushed in. I made things worse.*
>
> *Hank: Maggie was upset, and she was frustrated, and she lashed out at you. You only did what you thought was right to protect your sister. And no one can blame you for that.*

What was interesting about this conversation was that Maggie was described as upset and frustrated, but never wrong. Maggie was in fact completely right in her verbal accosting of Supergirl. The situation *was* made worse by Supergirl's approach and it did call for a different set of skills. However, instead of acknowledging these facts Hank Henshaw's response focused on relieving Supergirl's guilt. His statement "no one can blame you for that" is designed to make Supergirl feel better about her incorrect actions. The rationale he offers for why Supergirl should not feel guilty about her actions, is that she did what she thought was right. Supergirl actually had no reason for believing that her approach was right. In fact, it was quite the opposite. Before she left to take the incorrect actions, she was confronted by Maggie and given a justification for why they were the wrong actions to take. Instead of listening, Supergirl felt entitled to her belief with no justification. And when faced with her wrongness, she is immediately comforted with the idea that her belief and actions were okay because *she thought* they were right. Hank Henshaw basically tells Supergirl she should not have guilt around her actions, (she should be guiltless) because she believed they were the right actions to take. Even when they clearly weren't. The logic of Hank's statement goes something like this, Supergirl's belief in the rightness of her actions entitled her to have and act on those beliefs. And that belief in the rightness of her actions should also absolve her of guilt if those actions are wrong. Either way Supergirl should be guiltless because she did what she believed was right, even if there was no reason for her to believe that way. This is the second natural outcome of cognitive entitlement, guiltlessness.

The idea of guilt is an interesting one. Partly because it is often connected with shame. More accurately, it is often conflated with shame. Most of the research on morality and ethics over the years has focused on the two emotions of shame and guilt. Often using the terms synonymously. This misunderstanding of terms is regrettable because it often causes guilt to be associated with negative feelings that should be associated with shame and it prevents guilt from being used in its proper context and meaning. And guilt as it turns out is a fundamental component of ethics.

Over the years several scholars have tried to distinguish between the emotions of guilt and shame. One of the simplest and I think functional distinctions between the terms is the internal-external distinction. In this distinction, guilt is an internal process and shame is an external one. To be fair the debate about the distinction of these two terms is far more nuanced and detailed than this distinction allows, but this distinction creates a great framework by which to have a functional understanding of the difference between these two terms. In this distinction when an individual does (or thinks about doing) something ethically or morally wrong, guilt arises from their own internal cognitive processes and emotions. Guilt is not contingent on any social pressure or outside forces. It is an internal process. Whereas shame results from others discovering your wrong. Shame can only occur through an individual's interaction with others. It is based on social pressure and outside forces. In short, the distinction between guilt and shame is the distinction between feeling bad about doing something wrong because you were caught and others became aware of it (shame), or feeling bad for doing or thinking something wrong because it violates your own ethics (guilt). Utilizing this distinction is not only functional; it also makes it clear why historically guilt has been seen as the more useful of the two concepts in the study of ethics. In an article titled Moral Emotions and Moral Behavior the authors write, "guilt (verses shame) appears to be the more adaptive emotion, benefiting individuals and their relationships in a variety of ways"[10]. Many of these ways are directly linked to an individual's approach to ethics.

Ethics of course being the moral values, principles, and beliefs that govern a person's behavior and conduct. A person's ethics allow them to determine what is right and wrong, when it is right and wrong, how to respond when they do wrong, and how to act on those beliefs. The notion of guilt as an internal process links with an individual's ethics as it helps to form and shape these determinations. As an example a study by Taya Cohen of Carnegie Mellon University and two of her peers found that individuals who are more guilt prone (experience negative feelings of personal wrongdoing even when the wrongdoing is private) tend to be more ethical[11]. The researchers were examining the question "which individual differences—or *character traits*—predict people's unethical behavior". The answer they found was guilt proneness. In one experiment the researchers had 153 participants decide if they would take a promotion and a large pay increase by advising their organization to exploit a legal loophole and drill for oil in a country where drilling was made illegal due to human rights violations. The study found that While 41 percent of participants low in guilt proneness said they would probably or definitely exploit the loophole, only 25 percent of those with a high level of guilt proneness said the same. In another experiment, the researchers wanted to see if people would lie for monetary gain. Once again, they found that guilt proneness played a role in who lied and who didn't. The authors found that 45% of participants with low guilt proneness (don't feel guilt easily) lied to gain an extra $25 in the experiment, 36% of those who had medium guilt proneness lied to obtain the extra $25, and only 20% of those with high guilt proneness lied to get the extra $25. Cohen and team went on to find that guilt proneness played a role in dishonesty in negotiation,‘ "counterproductive work behaviors" defined as "volitional behavior that harms or is intended to harm organizations or people in organizations" (as an organizational scholar this one disturbs me), both work and general delinquency (this is also disturbing), and criminal behaviors. In each case, a person's guilt proneness was inversely related to their unethical behavior. The more guilt prone they were the more ethically they acted, and vice versa. The implication of Cohen's study is disturbing if in fact the culture is becoming "guiltless"

If Cohen and her team's research on unethical behavior is disturbing, then David Callahan's book *The Cheating Culture* is downright frightening[12]. While Cohen and team's research focused on percentages of groups with different levels of guilt proneness, Callahan's book looked at the increasing nature of cheating in the culture in general. What Callahan found was that there is a "profound moral crisis" occurring in the current culture[13]. People are "not only cheating more in many areas but they are also feeling less guilty about it"[14]. This lack of guilt is fueling a tidal wave, more accurately a monsoon of cheating and unethical behavior in the current culture. The sheer spectrum of cheating examples Callahan lays out are staggering. Callahan's book begins by telling the story of Municipal Credit Union (MCU) and the situation that led to over 4000 people overdrawing their accounts after 9/11. When its members recognized there was an issue with the reporting system at the MCU's ATM's, they took advantage and cheated the system. Millions of dollars ended up being taken. Even more troubling was the fact that many of MCU's customers were police officers and firefighters. The people society counts on for strong moral behavior. Callahan goes on to lay out situation after situation from investment bankers who knowingly lied to customers and the media. To whole corporate cultures of cheating, like Enron. However, the most alarming examples in Callahan's book are those of everyday citizens who have not only found ways to cheat, but have become completely guiltless regarding it. Consider two of Callahan's examples.

It is a felony to commit internet piracy of music and software. However in the early 2000's, and even currently, millions of people across the country have been and currently are illegally downloading music. Many of which according to Callahan have little to no guilt about it. In one of Callahan's interviews with a "music pirate" (his term not mine) Callahan said the person responded to the question "how do you justify your behavior" with the statement "I don't justify it, I haven't really thought about it". This statement implies both entitlement and guiltlessness The person didn't feel the need to make any justification for their thoughts on the subject or their actions (entitlement), and also didn't think about the impact of their actions, thus they had no guilt (guiltlessness).Similarly, Callahan employs the phenomenon of cable television theft as another example of cheating. According to Callahan at the time he wrote his book cable television theft accounted for over $6 billion in losses for cable companies per year (who knows what it is now). Callahan even shares the story of a police department that was receiving illegal cable. These are not career criminals, or people who are morally bankrupt.

This cheating is done by everyday individuals. In fact as one interviewee points out in Callahan's book "for many people this is the only illegal act they do". But they have become okay with this action because they are able to cognitively absolve themselves from guilt. Callahan' reports that a common rationale used by both "music pirates" and "cable thieves" (again his terms not mine) is that what they are doing is not wrong. That they are fighting back against corporate greed, or monopolies, or exacting revenge against tyrannical cable and music companies. Thus they are not the ones doing wrong, they are guiltless.

This rationale of being not guilty because the cheating actions are "sticking it to the man" or the fact that others don't even attempt to justify their actions, they just don't think about them; brings us back to the true danger of guiltlessness. Guiltlessness breeds malleable ethics. If you noticed I did not say that the result of guiltlessness was unethical behavior, I said it was malleable ethics. This is an important distinction. The thing that makes ethics, ethics, is that the person who holds them believes they are the right way to conduct themselves. Ethics are intrinsically and intimately connected to morality. A person bases their ethics on their morality. What they believe is right or wrong. Thus to cheat, or act unethical is to know that you are doing something wrong, and to do it anyway. To do something that you acknowledge is not moral. However, based on the examples provided by Callahan and the scene between Supergirl and Hank Henshaw, that is not what is happening with individuals. These individuals do not believe themselves to be acting unethical. In the case of Supergirl, she did not race off to try to save Alex knowing she wasn't being completely moral. That would have been unethical. Instead, when she flew off, she believed that she was being ethical. She was doing the moral thing.

Similarly, in Callahan's example of music and TV stealing, the interviewee's do not believe themselves to be acting unethical. They instead see themselves as moral champions. Countering the tyranny of corporate bureaucrats. They are not acting unethical, they are actually being quite moral in their minds. In these cases what is happening is that these individuals have malleable ethics. Their ethics are shifting to justify their actions and beliefs. Thus they are not violating their ethics they are still acting in accord with them. They have a malleable ethical code. Which I define as an ethical code that moves and changes for the individual based on what serves them best. An ethical code that can change what is seen as right and wrong based on how it affects the individual. It is a self-centered ethical code.

A point made by Tangney and company in their paper on morality explains why this is actually to be expected when an individual doesn't experience guilt. As the authors point out, guilt essentially leads to other-oriented empathy[15]. It causes individuals to think about the impact of their decision on others. Part of the strength of guilt proneness on ethical behavior is that it causes an individual to consider that their actions or beliefs may have harmed or can harm someone else. Guilt in an individual, forms a morality that considers the impact of wrong on others. Thus, an individual's ethic is not built on how that morality affects them only, but it also considers how it affects others as well. It focuses on a more collectivistic benefit. However, without guilt, an individual has lower levels of other oriented empathy. Their focus becomes more about individual benefit. In his book on cheating Callahan argues that one of the elements that has led to the cheating culture is rampant materialism, competitiveness, and greed. Individuals have begun focusing on how they can get more, benefit more, and obtain more. They are not as interested in how the actions needed to get more affect others. Callahan argues this leads them into cheating. I argue that they don't view it as cheating, they don't even view it as unethical. They instead are able to revise their ethics to make whatever benefits them the most not wrong. They are able to remain guiltless.

I actually started calling the current culture the guiltless culture well before I ran across Callahan's work or even considered cognitive entitlement. I actually began to call them the guiltless culture because of conversations I would have with teenagers and Millennials. I noticed that you couldn't guilt these individuals into changing their behavior or cognitions. They seemed impervious to guilt driven change. They were impervious to guilt driven change because they were impervious to guilt. I used to ask these groups things like "how do you feel about social media? Is it generally a good use of your time? Are the people polite on there?" To which they would reply that social media was a "time suck", the people were rude, there was bullying, etc. I would then ask them how often they were on social media, and how did they behave when online. Inevitably they would tell me that they were on social media constantly (in many cases they would tell me that they were on it while we were talking), and then give me a justification why they were not wrong when they acted rude or hurtful on social media. I would hear statements like "if somebody is coming at you online, you got to go at them, let them know, you know" (that's a quote, not my bad grammar). For those who don't speak Millennial or teenager, they were essentially saying that for them they had an ethic that allowed them to be mean and hurtful without being wrong. They had to protect themselves. They were not wrong, instead when they were being rude, they were being moral. So while it may be wrong for others it was not wrong for them. As another example, I once asked a group of young adults if it was

141

wrong to go to work late. They answered emphatically in the affirmative. "It is wrong to go to work late". I then asked them how often they go to work late. I was given answers like twice a week or three times a week. But these answers were again accompanied by a malleable ethic. When they went to work late it was because they knew that somebody else was already there, or that no customers would be there yet, etc. Once again it was wrong for others but not for them. As I conversed with more and more groups of young adults and youth I would find similar examples of malleable ethics around the music they listened to, how they viewed lying, and more. In each case, they were able to find a way for their actions to be ethically just. A way for them to not have to feel wrong, In essence, they found a way to be guiltless. And that guiltlessness allowed them to move their ethics as they saw fit. It allowed them to create malleable ethics.

Disappointment

While a decline in metacognition and the development of guiltlessness are unfortunate and ultimately damaging consequences of cognitive entitlement, they are not the most disheartening. In fact, the most discouraging of the consequences of cognitive entitlement is actually the impact that cognitive entitlement has on happiness. It is ironic but being entitled to your beliefs simply because you believe them to be right actually leads to higher levels of disappointment and psychological distress. You would think that an individual who is able to believe themselves right and not question their own beliefs would be an individual who would be genuinely happy. If as Schulz discussed in her book *Being Wrong: Adventures in the Margin of Error* being right brings human beings joy (see chapter 5), than an individual who doesn't have to justify being right in order to be right (cognitively entitled) should be an individual that is overall generally happy. That is why it is so discouraging that when it comes to entitlement, research has actually found the opposite.

One study that illustrates this finding was conducted by Joshua Grubbs and presented in the psychological bulletin in 2016. In his article, Grubbs and his team found that cognitive entitlement actually led to chronic disappointment and psychological distress for individuals[16]. Grubbs and his team reasoned that because of the way entitled individuals cognitively process expectations and information, they inadvertently cause themselves to be more disappointed and face more psychological distress. Grubbs and his team's assertion is based on the recognition that entitled individuals often have unrealistic expectations and beliefs. Meaning that their expectations and beliefs are often based on their perception and not external realities. This actually makes logical sense. If a person's, beliefs, and other cognitions are never allowed to be challenged externally, and internally they are not provided with a justification on why those beliefs and cognitions are valid, then there is nothing that forces those expectations to be grounded in reality. Internal justifications are what make us have to evaluate whether our beliefs correlate to reality. If a person believes they are an NBA caliber basketball player, in their 30's, after never having played basketball in college or since (I've played ball with a lot of these types of individuals). And, they reject external individuals who tell them they are not that good (they do, do this) the only thing left to tether them to reality is an internal justification. If they begin to ask themselves "why do I believe I am that good", they have to find evidence in reality to justify their belief. Things like how often their teams win, how many points they score, how often they can be stopped. This internal search for justification helps

143

them to view their beliefs in light of reality. Without this justification this person can believe themselves to be better than they are (this is how you end up with a scrub on your team taking 20 shots) and have unrealistic expectations for their performance. For me this in itself is a problem. I use the example of a basketball player, but imagine the stakes of unrealistic expectations for higher risk situations like cyber experts, investment bankers, or the president.

Grubbs and his team write that expectations, beliefs, and cognitions that do not correlate to reality lead to larger let downs when those cognitions are discovered to be wrong. This also seems to make logical sense. It is much easier to cope with the disappointment and psychological distress of being slightly wrong about a belief than it is to be massively wrong. Think about the times that you have taken a test in your life. In most cases, it was probably easier to deal with the disappointment and psychological distress of not doing as well as you thought, when you expected to not do well on the test. If you expected to get a "C" because you know you didn't prepare well and you receive a "C-" or a high "D" you are probably disappointed but probably not as much as if you expected to get an "A" and received a "C-" or "D". In the latter situation you would probably face a more intense level of disappointment and psychological distress. This is what occurred in the Supergirl episode. Before she left to "save her sister", Supergirl had the expectation (though not tethered to reality) that she would fly off and rescue her sister. Upon recognizing that she made the situation worse, Supergirl is confronted with strong disappointment and psychological distress. The mismatch between her expectations and what actually occurred created a large disappointment gap. This is what Grubbs and his teams argue is occurring with individuals who are cognitively entitled. These individuals live in such a way

144

that their cognitions, beliefs, and expectations are much higher than they would be if those elements were grounded in reality. Because they feel entitled to those cognitions and don't have to offer a justification based on external realities or internal processing they can have cognitions that are further from reality. But when actual outcomes occur that differ from these cognitions these individuals will face higher levels of disappointment and psychological distress. Just like the test-taking example, the reality of the results leads to a larger disappointment gap with these individuals. Thus, they are constantly and chronically disappointed and have much higher levels of psychological distress.

This phenomenon of mismatching expectations and the associated disappointment and psychological distress is being written about quite extensively in the current organizational literature. Organizational scholars are writing in great depth about employees and organizational members entering organizations with elevated expectations around salary, benefits, work-life balance and more. Similarly, many new employees are blogging about their disappointment in how organizations are offering overly restrictive work environments, low pay, and lack of work-life balance. In most cases, the mismatching of expectations, disappointment, and psychological distress in organizations is being attributed to generational differences. Millennials versus generation Z versus generation X, versus the Baby Boomers. And while I certainly think generational differences are a factor, I also believe that it is less about generational differences and more about entitlement and its infusion into culture. Those individuals who have embraced the Hater Mindset will likely have different expectations and cognitions than what may really occur in the world. Thus, they are more prone to higher levels of disappointment and psychological distress when those expectations are not met. This doesn't matter if they are Millennials, Generation Z, Generation X, or Baby Boomers. Entitlement, as Grubbs and his team point out, leads to entitled cognitions. Which ultimately results in disappointment and psychological distress.

However, mismatched expectations are not the only element that leads to unhappiness in cognitively entitled individuals. According to a different study on entitlement, entitlement not only leads to chronic disappointment and psychological distress, it also leads to interpersonal relationship problems. A study published in the Journal of Experimental Social Psychology found that "entitled people create conflict and hostility in their relationships"[17]. The authors found that for entitled individuals, relationship conflict is chronic and continuous. This conflict has a two-fold impact. The first is that it causes higher levels of unhappiness in individuals, because meaningful relationships have been found to be the number one most important factor in individual happiness. We will touch on this in the next chapter. The second thing that it does is that it causes individuals to place less emphasis, and commitment on relationships. They begin to value relationships less. Which is actually the third outcome of the "Hater Mindset", The Hater Mindset leads to the devaluing of relationships.

Summary

I began this section on the "you" in the "you are just a hater" sentence examination by pointing out how "you" in the Hater Mindset is actually a projection. The person using the phrase "you are just a hater" is actually projecting the fear of being wrong onto another individual. They are preserving their self-image by pushing the idea that they are wrong away from themselves. This in turn leads to cognitive entitlement. An individual who can always push the idea that they are wrong on to someone else never has to offer a justification for their beliefs. They can simply choose to believe them and whenever confronted with the possibility of their beliefs wrongness, they can project that possibility on to someone else. Which in itself does not initially seem like such a bad thing. Especially in today's culture. Common cultural language today is that people can believe whatever they want to believe. That there need not be a justification for what you believe, you just need to believe it. However, in this chapter I hoped to point out why this line of thinking is flawed. If a person need not explain or justify what they believe they will have no need for metacognition, they will face no feelings of guilt, and they set themselves up for potentially higher levels of disappointment. All of which are not things that lead to the optimal functioning of an individual or our current culture.

PART 4 –"JUST A"

Chapter 8 –Me, Myself, and I… Are So Alone

"Uh, I'm sorry I didn't know I was supposed to care"
-Internet Meme

In 2015, the psychiatrist Robert Waldinger shared a TED Talk on the Harvard Study for Adult Development. At first glance, this seemingly unremarkable and highly academic study would appear to be of little interest for the general public. Which is why it is surprising that in 2017 Waldinger's talk had been viewed over 15 million times. One appeal of Waldinger's talk may be its title. The talk isn't titled an overview on the Harvard Study of Adult Development, but is more aptly and more accurately titled "What Makes a Good Life: Lessons from the longest study on happiness"[1]. As it turns out the talk isn't about an unremarkable scientific study but it discusses the longest study on humans in modern history. In his talk, Waldinger outlines how the Harvard Study of Adult Development, of which he is the latest director, has tracked the lives of 724 men for 78 years. The researchers surveyed the men every two years about their physical and mental health, their professional lives, friendships, and marriages. They also conducted blood tests, medical exams, brain scans, and periodic interviews. Waldinger argues that the results of the study have much to say about happiness and what makes a good life. The major premise of Waldinger's talk, and in my opinion, probably one of the most fascinating findings of scientific research is summarized in his statement "good relationships keep us happier and healthier. Period". The Harvard Study identified good relationships as a fundamental and foundational element of human happiness. Good relationships, being meaningful ones, add deeply to our lives. After 78 years of studying human beings, Waldinger concludes that the true key to happiness is meaningful relationships.

Waldinger's talk made me begin to think deeply about relationships in the current culture. And what role the Hater Mindset might have on relationships. Waldinger began his talk by citing the results of a recent survey on individuals in the culture and what they identified as their most important life goals. In the survey 80% of participants stated that one of their most important life goals was to get rich, and 50% stated that one of their most important life goals was to become famous. This means that the majority of participants in the study identified elements outside of relationships as the goals they thought were most important to them. These survey results point to a strong disconnect between what the current culture identifies as the things they believe will help them have a good life, and the results found through the Harvard Study of Adult Development. While the Harvard Study of Adult Development calls for an increasing emphasis on relationships. The current culture seems to place less emphasis on them. This deemphasizing of relationships I argue is indicative of the "just a" approach to relationships. An approach that devalues relationships. And a natural outcome of the Hater Mindset.

Shortly after watching Waldinger's TED talk, I thought about three separate situations that demonstrated the connection between the Hater Mindset and relationships. The first was a story shared with me about an acquaintance of mine (we'll call him Tom) and the actions he took after the 2015 NBA finals. Tom was an avid LeBron James fan, and after the finals a friend of mine (will call him Jim) noticed Tom working furiously, frustratingly, and aggressively on Facebook. Since

Facebook is not usually associated with these three things (people are normally casually browsing, happily, and calmly) Jim asked Tom what he was doing. Tom stated that after the conclusion of the finals he was deleting anyone he knew who was a Golden State Warriors fan from his friends list. When asked why, he stated that he didn't want to see anything about how good the Warriors were and how LeBron James lost (he was avoiding dissent, this was discussed in chapter 4). Jim asked Tom if he was worried that he may lose contact with some of his friends by deleting them, to which Tom replied. "I still have over 1000 friends. If they are a Golden State Warriors fan I don't need them as a friend".

The second situation that occurred was between a co-worker (we'll call him Sam) and I. It was in 2016 during the highly contentious presidential campaign. Sam and I were talking about the upcoming holiday and what we were going to do to celebrate. When I asked Sam what his plans were he told me that he wasn't sure. He would normally go to his mother's house for the holiday, but recently he and his mother had not been speaking. Unsolicited, (you know that means he was an over sharer) Sam went on to explain how he and his mother had come into conflict around the candidates for the 2016 election. Apparently, Sam's mother had declared that she was going to vote for a candidate that Sam did not support and this had put such a strain on their relationship that the two hadn't talked in months. I am paraphrasing, but at one point in the conversation, Sam said something along the lines of, "if she is going to align herself with those views I can't understand how we can even be around each other, let alone have a relationship".

The third situation that occurred transpired with a family member of mine (we'll call him Michael). In this situation, Michael was in an online group discussion with members of a service based Greek organization of which

153

he was a member. For those unfamiliar with these types of Greek organizations, they are not only founded on service, but also on brotherhood and sisterhood. The members of these organizations are usually characterized by strong relationships, often referring to each other as brother and sister. In this particular case, the online discussion group was composed of members from various cohort years. One day a debate arose in the online discussion group that encompassed a very controversial topic. One of the group members and Michael ended up taking opposite sides on this controversial issue. This is not uncommon. What happen next was not uncommon either, but it is still shocking. As the conversation progressed, the rhetoric of Michael and the other member of the group begin to turn contentious. Other members of the group began to jump in on both sides of the argument and in the end the group-member announced that the discussion group was in fact full of "strangers" and left the discussion group altogether. Apparently the conversation had become so frustrating for the group member that they no longer wanted to use language that portrayed the other group members as family (brother and sister), and instead chose to label them as "strangers".

The three situations I thought about were all similar in that they encompassed elements of the Hater Mindset that have been previously discussed. The individuals in these situations were not tolerant of or open to dissent. And they also chose to think that others were the problem, ignored the possibility that they may be wrong, and felt entitled to their beliefs. However, these situations also had one more thing in common. The individuals involved in them seem to place little value on the relationships that were being changed or impacted due to their differing opinions. In the case of the first situation, the individual had no concerns that he may be removing, changing, or even destroying friendships simply because they had a different view on the outcome of an NBA game. In the second situation, this individual was willing to sever a relationship with their mother, arguably the first meaningful relationship in their life, because they differed on political candidates. And in the third situation one individual was willing to turn individuals from brothers and sisters to "strangers" in a matter of moments because of their differing perspectives (and to be fair the delivery of those perspectives) on a controversial issue. These three situations, I think are representative of the third outcome of the Hater Mindset. **A devaluing of relationships.** Individuals who follow the Hater Mindset place less value on relationships in general. And allocate even lower levels of value to relationships when dissent or conflict is involved. People who have embraced the Hater Mindset are willing to damage or even destroy existing relationships over dissent. They are likely to declare, "you are *just a* hater".

The phrase "just a" in the "you are just a hater" sentence is one of my favorite to examine. Mostly because at first glance the phrase seems to be insignificant. Without examining it or placing an emphasis on it, the phrase looks like an unneeded modifier that adds little to the meaning of the sentence. The sentence "You are a hater" would appear to work just as well (see what I did there "just" as well). But in truth, the phrase "just a" actually adds significantly to the sentence. In fact, it adds a completely new implicit idea to the phrase. One that I believe exposes how the Hater Mindset views relationships, especially those relationships that are facing dissent.

When someone uses the phrase "just a" they are usually substituting it for merely or only. The phrase "just a" is like saying it is "only a" or it is "merely a". The phrase typically has two ideas implicitly linked to it. The first is a lack of uniqueness. The phrase "just a" implies

155

that whatever is being referenced is not original, novel, or special. It is generic, regular, or ordinary. Take for an example "that's just a No. 2 Pencil". The phrase "just a" signifies that No. 2 Pencils are a dime a dozen. There is nothing unique, special, or novel about them. They are just like all the other No. 2 pencils. In fact the idea of ordinary and regular is so connected to the phrase "just a" that when someone applies it to something we know isn't ordinary or regular, we perceive them as being either sarcastic, facetious, or pretentious. Take for example if you were to hear someone say, "oh, that's just a gold supercharged Lamborghini Diablo with suicide doors" or "oh that, that's just a Ming Dynasty vase". In both cases the term "just a" doesn't seem to fit because it denotes ordinary and regular. And neither a Lamborghini Diablo nor a Ming Dynasty vase are things you would see regularly or ordinarily. We would perceive the person who said these sentences as either joking, being facetious, or more likely pretentions. And we would feel this way, because a lack of uniqueness is connected to the phrase "just a". We would believe the person using it for something unique would have to be aware of this inherent contradiction.

In the same way that ordinariness is inherent to the phrase "just a", a lack of value is also intrinsically linked to the phrase. When someone says something is "just a", beyond saying the thing is not special they are also saying that the thing they are referencing is not valuable. I'm not talking about monetary value here; I'm talking about value to the individual speaking. Someone may say, "it's just a car". In this case, the car may have monetary value, but what the person is saying is that the car doesn't have significant value to them. They don't think of it as important or irreplaceable. The car in this scenario is not something that should be worried about, or that great effort (physical or emotional) should be expended over. This example demonstrates how the phrase "just a" in addition to communicating a lack of novelty or uniqueness also communicates a lack of value.

At this point I hope that it is clear why I think that the phrase "just a" is a problem in the "you are just a hater" sentence and the Hater Mindset. The sentence "you are just a hater" is being directed at another human being. It is applying the same two inherent meanings of lack of novelty, originality, and uniqueness and lack of value, to another person. It is in essence telling another human being that they are not unique or special, and as such, they are not valued by the person speaking. They don't necessitate the effort needed or required for something that is valuable. The person saying this sentence to another person (whether they are doing it intentionally or not) is actually communicating meanings to both the other person (the labeled) and themselves (the labeler). The labeler is communicating to the labeled that they don't consider them or their opinion as special, unique, or valued. In addition, the labelers are communicating to themselves that the labeled person in this conversation is replaceable. There is no reason to value them as unique and special or to apply effort to this relationship. This person can just be replaced. Just like the person who was deleting people from his Facebook for being Golden State Warriors fans, the Hater Mindset leads individuals to believe relationships are replaceable. When asked if he was afraid that he might be losing contact with friends, the Facebook deleter said I still have over 1000 friends. What he was really saying is that those relationships that I'm losing are replaceable, so I don't need to worry about them. They are not unique and they are not valued.

There are several dangers, in my view, of approaching relationships with a "just a" mindset. One of the most significant of these dangers is the impact it can potentially have on individuals having happy lives. This approach to relationships is opposite of the one advocated for by the Harvard Study of Adult Development. Thus one of the dangers of viewing relationships with a "just a" mindset is that it can potentially impact a person's potential for happiness at the individual level. The second danger is much more expansive to the overall culture and will be discussed further in the next chapter. It focuses on the idea that to view another human being as replaceable, as ordinary, and not valuable or cheap, is to strip them of their human worth. And to do this because of dissent is to dehumanize them because of their differing perspective. This I believe can have a dramatic impact on the world and behavior of people if integrated into the culture.

At this point two logical questions arise. The first is, is there any real evidence that the Hater Mindset leads to a devaluing of relationships. I have argued that the Hater Mindset creates a "just a" approach to relationships. I offered some anecdotal evidence, but the question remains, do people actually view relationships this way in the current culture? The second question that arises is why the Hater Mindset would lead to a devaluing of relationships. Yes the phrase "just a" implies devaluing, but what about the Hater Mindset leads it to devalue relationships? Why does the mindset produce a "just a" approach in the first place?

In answering the first question, I think there is significant evidence that the Hater Mindset is leading to a devaluing of relationships. That evidence is that individuals in the current culture report having smaller numbers of relationships in general and fewer meaningful ones than previous generations. In his talk on relationships Waldinger references both the amount and quality of relationships as factors for happiness. He says "it turns out that people who are more socially connected to family, to friends, to community, are happier, they're physically healthier, and they live longer…"[2] However, he also references the quality of those relationships. Waldinger says, "it's not just the number of friends you have, and it's not whether or not you're in a committed relationship, but it's the quality of your close relationships that matter"[3]. For Waldinger both the number of relationships and the quality of those relationships are important for happiness. Studies done on the current culture report lower levels of both of these. According to the General Social Survey, the number of people who report that they have no close friends has tripled since 1985[4]. And while most people used to report having 3 close friends they can talk to about "important matters" that number has now fallen to 2. On top of that, more people report feeling lonely and isolated. Indicating less total connections and even less meaningful ones. I argued earlier that the Hater Mindset seems to be coming to its apex in Millennials and Generation Z. If it is true that the Hater Mindset causes individuals to devalue relationships then evidence should show similar issues of fewer relationships and less meaningful relationships highly present in these two generations. And although little research has been done on Generation Z (they are still coming of age) surveys on their relationships indicate that they do tend to have less meaningful relationships and fewer deeper connections. While the General Social Survey found that loneliness seems to be most prevalent in Millennials. Millennials report lower levels of relationships in general and lower levels of close meaningful relationships as well[5]. At the same time Millennials are reporting that the things most important to them are not friendships and relationships but money and fame. This combination of factors seems to provide convincing evidence that relationships are not as much a priority in current culture as they have been historically or even as they should be today. Relationships are being devalued.

This leads to the second logical question about the "just a" approach and devaluing relationships. Why would the Hater Mindset lead to a devaluing of relationships? Why would the way people deal with dissent cause them to view relationships differently? In answering this question I think Millennials themselves have been quite insightful. An article written for the Huffington Post in 2016 by blogger and Millennial Krysti Wilkinson proclaims, "we want the facade of a relationship, but we don't want the work of a relationship"[6]. Wilkinson's article was ironically entitled *"We Are the Generation that Doesn't want Relationships"*. Her point was that relationships in the current culture have become more surfacy and shallow than deep and meaningful. Individuals want to appear to be connected to others, but are not interested in genuinely putting in the effort to achieve meaningful relationships. They don't see the value. A separate article *titled "12 Reasons That Meaningful Relationships are Becoming More and More Rare"* written for the website Thought Catalog by author Brianna Wiest, makes two observations I think are also relevant[7]. She writes, "we think that people are consumable" (meaning easy to obtain and dismiss, like a product) and "we think meaning is something we find not something we create (meaning it doesn't require effort)". Wiest point hearkens back to the three situations I mentioned earlier. In those three situations the people involved treated relationships as consumable. Things that could be picked up or dismissed based on the feelings a person has at the time. They were consumable in the same way that No. 2 pencils are consumable. Valued only until they are not needed anymore. The people in the three situations mentioned earlier did not endeavor to maintain the relationships through conflict and disagreement. They didn't think that

160

the relationships were worth the effort. Because they required just that, "effort". This point made by Wilkinson and Wiest is the same one that Waldinger mentions during his TED talk. Waldinger says, "relationships are messy and they're complicated and the hard work of tending to family and friends, is not sexy or glamorous." Waldinger uses the term hard work in the same way that Wiest and Wilkinson do, to reference what it takes to develop meaningful relationships. Meaningful relationships don't just occur they are worked at. And the reason they must be worked at is because meaningful relationships include dissent. Dissent often manifests itself in conflict, disagreement, and differing opinions. And that conflict, disagreement, and differing of opinions explains why meaningful relationships are not characteristic of the Hater Mindset and why the Hater Mindset leads to a devaluing of relationships.

As was discussed earlier the Hater Mindset does not engage with dissent or disagreement. It avoids it. Dissent causes the Hater Mindset to doubt its rightness, to doubt its self-image, and thus it chooses not to engage dissent. It dismisses it. The problem is that dissent is characteristic of close and meaningful relationships. The neuroscientist Harriet Braiker and social psychologist Harold Kelley make this point in a chapter they authored together titled "Conflict in the Development of Close Relationships"[8]. Braiker and Kelley point out that the nature of a close relationship raises the potential for dissent, conflict, disagreement, and differing opinions. They write, "a person that has no special interest in another has no conflict", but when individuals have significant interest or value in each other they have higher potential for conflict and disagreement on multiple levels. Braiker and Kelley lay out conflict and disagreement that occurs at an interpersonal level, at an interdependence level, and even conflict and disagreement about personal characteristics and attitudes. These are all types of conflict and disagreement that are likely to occur in close and meaningful relationships. Therein lies the problem and the paradox for the Hater Mindset. The Hater Mindset does not deal well with conflict, dissent or disagreement, but those things are necessary parts of meaningful relationships. We learned earlier that when the brain needs to hold two conflicting cognitions it causes cognitive dissonance. The person with dissonance must find a way to relieve the cognitive tension that is occurring. In this case, the Hater Mindset individual must choose. They must choose between the desire to disdain and dismiss dissent, or the choice to face the dissent, conflict, and disagreement and the challenge it poses to their self-image, for the sake of maintaining the relationship. They must choose which they value more. The result is that the Hater Mindset takes the "just a" approach to relationships and chooses to devalue, change, or sever the relationships rather than deal with the dissonance caused by them.

The Hater Mindset is able to sever these relationships because of the three elements associated with a "just a" approach. First, the Hater Mindset labels the relationship as ordinary and replaceable. And just like the acquaintance of mine who deleted all of his Facebook friends knowing he had "1000 more", the Hater Mindset loses the uniqueness of each relationship. After it labels the relationships as ordinary and replaceable it then places less value on them, just like the situation where my co-worker chose to sever the relationship with their mother, arguably one of the most important relationships in an individual's life, rather than work through the conflict. And finally, the Hater Mindset hinders the individual from putting forth the effort to work through disagreement and conflict and develop stronger meaningful relationships. Just like the third situation with the person who labeled his Greek organization brothers and sisters "strangers" and left the group, the Hater Mindset doesn't think it is worth the effort. These three steps allow the person with the Hater Mindset to go one-step further than devaluing the relationship. It allows them to devalue the person in general. Since they no longer value the relationship with the individual, they no longer need to value the individual. If the relationship with the individual is not special, not unique, not valued, then neither is the person the relationship was connected to. In other words, these three steps by the Hater Mindset allow an individual to do what I refer to in this book as "dehumanize the dissenter". It is to this dehumanization that I now turn.

Chapter 9 – I Am Legend! You Are A Zombie

"Typical human behavior is now entirely absent"
-Robert Neville from I am legend
(Will Smith's Character)

During my time working as an educational life coach for a non-profit educational organization in the Midwest, I was challenged to teach my 7th, 8th, and 9th graders about compassion. As anyone who has ever worked with teenagers can probably tell you, teenagers are not necessarily the most compassionate people on the Earth. They are more, what's the word…cruel. Yeah, that's the word, cruel. A teenager's sense of empathy in most cases does not seem to be fully developed and they are usually not shy about demonstrating this fact. Teenagers are constantly finding ways to show their lack of compassion. Whether that is by laughing at individuals who fell and hurt themselves, or in more dire circumstances standing by and making jokes like the teenagers who filmed a man drowning. Teenagers and empathy are not usually congruent phenomenon. And at the same time that teenagers have underdeveloped senses of empathy they are also in the midst of developing their cognitive independence. Meaning that they do not just accept statements that claim to be true as actually true. This combination makes teaching compassion to them a challenge. You can't just walk in to a room full of teenagers and say that it is important that you are compassionate and believe they will then be compassionate, agree it's needed, or think you are right. The teenager's immediate reply would be to ask you "why". Why do you need to be compassionate and why is it wrong to be rude or cruel to others? Especially if you don't like them? So my teaching partner and I knew that in order to convey this information effectively and for it to be impactful for our students we would have to provide some context for our compassion lesson.

We decided to begin with a central tenant and idea and work backwards from there. The central tenant or idea we chose was the belief that killing another human being was wrong. This may seem like an odd place to start, but the idea was to scaffold back to compassion from a generally accepted idea. Most people (even teenagers, for the most part) will argue that killing another human being is wrong. My teaching partner and I specified that we were talking about killing, not self-defense or any other unique situation, but to blatantly take another person's life is wrong. To this point most of the students agreed. We then asked the question "why". Why is it wrong to take the life of a human being? After several discussions around punishment and feeling bad, we centered on the idea that every human has value by nature of them existing. They have what we called "human worth". They have value because they are a unique, one of a kind, human individual. The concept of human worth is built on the idea that humans are unique, and have significant value to each other. They are not "just a".

This central tenant if followed bridges out into multiple different notions. If every human being has value or worth than they should be given a measure of respect for their human worth. In the same way, if every human being has human worth, than we should generally be civil to each other because we value each other. We should at least attempt to empathize with each other, because we are having similar human experiences. And from this empathy we should have compassion on each other. As we try to understand each other's perspective in empathy we should also have concern for others and their sufferings. Which as it turns out is the very definition of compassion. And this was the approach we used. An approach that was built on human worth. The idea that humans have intrinsic value and that value necessitates civility, empathy, respect, compassion, and a host of other noble behaviors toward our fellow man.

The question we didn't ask in our classes was, but what happens if the idea of human worth disappears? What happens if a person is somehow stripped of their human worth or value? This is a question that philosophers have wrestled with for decades and recently zombie or diseased human movies like *World War Z*, *I Am Legend*, and shows like *The Walking Dead* have explored in depth. Over the past few years I have been enamored with the paradox of zombies that you see in zombie movies and shows. The whole premise of these movies and shows is the loss of human value or worth. Consider one of my favorite examples of this, the movie *I Am Legend* (or insert your favorite zombie movie here). In this film the main character, Robert Neville played by Will Smith, is able to witness the outbreak of an epidemic that changes humans into zombie like creatures. Robert Neville who remains unaffected is then thrown into a world where these former humans have been stripped of their humanity and thus their human worth. At one point in the movie when describing the new creatures he says the quote that began this chapter, "typical human behavior is now entirely absent". Meaning that the creatures that Neville now interacts with are no longer considered human. They are no longer unique or have human value. As a result of viewing them this way, we see Neville's behavior toward these creatures change dramatically.

At the beginning of the *I am Legend* movie Neville is a scientist working to better mankind, with no desire to harm others. By the end of the movie he is able to kill zombie like humans with no remorse. We as the audience members watch and don't even blink as Will Smith strategically tricks the zombie characters into a scenario that results in him running hundreds of them over with his car. And we even cheer at the end of the movie as thousands of the zombies are killed in a massive explosion. After their transformation from human to zombie we don't expect Neville to be civil, to have respect for, or to attempt to bond with these creatures. We are okay with him despising them because they are not human. At one point the viewer finds out that Neville has been experimenting on the zombie creatures and experimenting in such a way that some of them end up dying. This discovery however does not lead to a sense of sadness or loss for the zombie creatures, only for the failure of the experiments. However, in the midst of all this behavior what is important to note is that these zombies were once humans. At the beginning of the movie before their transitions from human to zombie we would have cringed at the idea of a person indiscriminately killing them. The film would have to be considered a horror film if the main character was experimenting on human beings while they were alive and causing many of them to die. And there would likely have been protests at theaters over a scene where a car drives through a crowd of people at full speed, with protesters claiming it too closely resembles real life situations. But none of that occurred (or does occur). And the reason why is because the zombie characters in these movies and shows are not viewed as humans but as less than. And since they are less than humans they don't have to be afforded respect, civility, or compassion. In fact, they don't even have to be valued. Their dehumanization causes the loss of their human worth in the mind of Robert Neville, the other characters, and even the movie or show watcher.

The examination of the "I AM LEGEND" movie is insightful because it gives us an idea of what happens when an individual dehumanizes another person in their mind. It answers the question what happens when an individual no longer sees another as having human worth or value. When people begin to see themselves as "I am Legend" and other as zombies. And understanding this is important because dehumanization is what I propose is happening as a result of the "just a" approach to relationships and dissent in the current culture.

In 1999, the conservative scholar Paul Gottfried coined the term the dehumanization of dissent (henceforth referred to as DOD) as a way to describe a phenomenon he noticed in society[1]. Gottfried observed that individuals in society were choosing a unique method of argumentation to deal with conservative dissent. Instead of focusing on countering an individual's arguments or points, people were labeling individuals as bigots, haters, or other negative names. And this was becoming the preferred way to respond to conservative dissent. Gottfried described this labeling as "dehumanizing". It is important to note that Gottfried was not using dehumanization in the sense of actually portraying people as less than human. People were not arguing that their dissenters were apes or monsters(or maybe they were). What Gottfried meant by dehumanizing was to portray a person as not like you, to portray them as someone who does not warrant human decency, respect, or civility because they don't have it themselves. To dehumanize by Gottfried's definition is to portray someone as disconnected from the humanity in others, namely "me". It is essentially to say, "that this person is not like me". Gottfried argued that by portraying dissenters this way, people were attempting to simultaneously invalidate the dissenter's opinions, perspectives, and even the dissenters themselves.

169

Although I don't agree with some of Gottfried's political perspectives, his description of DOD parallels much of what has been described in this book so far. In fact, the sentence "you are just a hater" could actually be described as an attempt at DOD. The person using this sentence hopes to label the other person as "a hater" and thus invalidate their opinion and even the individual themselves, portraying them as without decency or without humanity. They are instead "just a hater". And the term "hater" as was established earlier is not like "me". The term "hater" does not denote compassion, decency, or humanity. It denotes the opposite. It makes sure that whoever is called a hater I recognize as "not like Me", they are separate from me. They are dehumanized because of their dissent.

While Gottfried's concept is relevant for an individual's behavior toward dissent, I also think it apropos for the larger culture as well. Gottfried's concept begs the question what happens when this approach to relationships, this DOD, becomes embedded into the culture of a society. As I referenced back in chapter 2, when I say culture I am referring to the concept of culture as defined in organizational theory. The idea that culture represents the "correct way to perceive, think, and feel" that is taught to others as the correct way to perceive, think, and feel". What happens when the correct way to perceive, think, and feel about dissent is to dehumanize the dissenter? When this is the approach that is taught to others as they way to handle dissent? To dehumanize it. This I believe is when we find ourselves in the culture of "I AM LEGEND and you are a zombie". When dissent causes me to no longer view you like me, and to treat you accordingly. This is where I believe the film *I am Legend* can be helpful. The film offers several excellent parallels for how a culture and society will act if DOD becomes the correct way to perceive, think or feel about dissent.

Us and Them

One of the first parallels that can be drawn from *I AM LEGEND* is how dehumanization leads to polarization. Early in the movie when the virus that changes humans into zombies is beginning to spread, Neville and his family are driving out of the city when suddenly a zombie like creature jumps onto the side of their moving vehicle. The face of the zombie is distorted and changed and looks much different than Neville, his wife, and daughter. It is obviously diseased. This scene serves to paint a stark contrast between Neville and family, the humans, and the zombie characters. It introduces what is known in social psychology as an in-group and an out-group for the Neville character. In social psychology the idea of an in-group is a group to which a member feels psychologically a part. In-groups represent similarity and comfort. In contrast, an out-group is a group in which an individual does not identify. Individuals feel distanced or disconnected from out-groups. They represent dis-similarity and discomfort. In the car scene, the movie watcher can immediately see that Neville is not like the zombie creatures, while *he is* like his wife and child. It is clear that there are two separate groups and Neville is a part of one and not the other. This is the first step of dehumanization and polarization. Distinction from another person or group. However, the simple existence of in groups and out-groups does not necessarily lead to polarization. Simply having in groups and out-groups does not make those groups polarized from each other or even opposed to each other. I disagree with those who think Superman is a great superhero. They are obviously in my out-group (they gave him too many powers: flight, x-ray, heat vision, super-hearing, freeze breath, strength, and so on. I mean really, really). But despite this I do not feel polarized from them. We can still find a way to agree with each other, build common ground, and work together.

However, the portrayal of in groups and out-groups is not all that occurs in the scene with Neville his family and the car. Something else happens when the zombie creature jumps on the car that *can* lead to polarization. When the creature jumps on the car Neville loses control of the steering wheel and his daughter begins screaming something about a monster. This is a pivotal scene because it takes the in-group out-group dichotomy to the next level. The out-group now not only exists, but it is a danger to the Neville family. It is harmful or has the potential to be harmful to the in-group. This view of harm from the out-group moves the out-group from simply being different to being dangerous. From being separate to being enemies. If an out-group poses a danger to the in-group than no longer are they just separate from the in-group they are against it. And while it may be easy to seek out common ground with someone different, it is much harder to do so with someone you perceive as an enemy. In fact when an out-group is perceived as an enemy, because of their potential harm to the in-group, it is much easier to focus on how you are different from them than it is to focus on how you may be the same.

This is what we see from Neville later in the film. About a quarter way into the movie after interacting with some of the zombie creatures (who I would argue had just shown a similarity with Neville), Neville makes a video journal where he says the statement that began this chapter. "Typical human behavior is now entirely absent". Neville's quote here signifies that he no longer sees any similarity with the zombie like creatures and himself. He can't even identify an area where he and the creatures may be alike. The zombie creatures represent harm to his in-group, (his family was killed by them and presumably all of humanity as well) and because of that they are his enemies. He seeks no common ground with them. He is polarized against them. To agree with them or be like them is, in his words to be entirely absent of human behavior. So since he can't be like them he must be against them.

This description is what I mean when I say polarization. It means to believe that you can't be like the out-group for fear that it means you are dehumanized like them. Thus, you must be against them. To agree with them would somehow bring you to their level. Which is a level that is dehumanized. I would argue that this description of polarization accurately describes American politics for at least the past decade and probably longer.

The American political system is often described as polarized. As a country individuals have outlined their in groups, whether those are liberals or conservatives, social justice advocates or Americanism supporters, Republicans or Democrats. And they have dehumanized their out-groups. In a 2016 TED talk on how divided we are as a country the psychologist Jonathan Haidt points out that we often now look at those who differ from us with disgust[2]. Not simply with disagreement but with disgust. And disgust he says paints people as "subhuman, monstrous, deformed, morally deformed". His description parallels the viewing of out-groups as not simply out-groups but as enemies. We are disgusted by out-groups. We can't be like them at all, because that would mean we are like them, we are not human, we are subhuman, monstrous, deformed, morally deformed.

In fact, polarization has become so much engrained into American politics that to *not* hear it often sounds odd. While listening to the radio in 2017 I heard a democratic senator discussing a recent event around racism that had occurred. The reporter asked the senator whether he was surprised some of his republican peers spoke out against the event. The senator responded by saying "no" he wasn't surprised, many of the republicans he serves with are his friends and he expected them to also be outraged by racism. The comment was so out of the ordinary and so unexpected that I pulled my car over and began researching the senator immediately. I was so used to hearing polarized views that to hear such civility, respect, and belief in good intentions of the out-group (to be discussed later in this chapter) made me want to research this senator right away (in order to avoid the appearance that I am campaigning for anyone I haven't put the senator's name here. I know you wanted to know though).

The depth of polarization of out-groups in our culture really hit home for me while watching TV one night. I was watching a late night commentator discuss the controversy and uproar between the "black lives matter" and "blue lives matter" movements. During his discussion the commentator made this statement, "if I say that black lives matter, that doesn't mean that I am automatically saying that blue lives don't". This statement hit home to me not because the commentator said it, but because they felt the need to say it. The commentator felt they had to preface their statement by saying just because I make this statement doesn't mean I am a part of one group and against another. The commentator was essentially saying, by making this statement I am not your enemy. I am not different from you. As I watched this statement I recognized the depth that polarization had taken in American political culture. We are so polarized that to make a statement means that you are aligning yourself with an enemy out-group or friend in-group. To say "black lives matter" and "blue lives matter" is to cause some people cognitive dissonance. Because to them the two views are polarized, opposite, enemies. This is one of the outcomes of dehumanization. It leads us to be polarized, steeped further into our position because to

174

agree at all with the dissenters is to be like the group that has been dehumanized for that dissent. It is to be as inhuman as they are.

Intentions, Communication, and Empathy

The problem with polarization, besides the fact that it is just wrong, is that it encumbers an individual's ability to empathize with members of the out-group. People who are polarized from others are less likely to empathize with those they have dehumanized because dehumanization obscures an individual's ability to see nobility in the intentions of the out-group members. And impedes communication between the two polarized groups, making it harder to understand the perspective of the out-group members. To understand these points we return to "I AM LEGEND".

The scene where Neville states, "typical human behavior is entirely absent" actually follows a peculiar sequence of events. In the movie the zombie like creatures are vulnerable to sunlight. In fact, exposure to sunlight is damaging even to the point of death. Before Neville makes the statement that began this chapter he sets a trap to capture a female zombie creature. Upon her being captured a male zombie creature voluntarily exposes himself to the light to shriek a monstrous yell at Neville. The scene appears to suggest to the movie watcher that the male zombie was angry with the female zombie being taken. Which would be typical human behavior. However, in his video notes on the events Neville does not even consider anger by the male zombie over the female zombie being taken as a possible option for why the male zombie would voluntarily expose himself to sunlight. Instead, he proposes decreased brain function and scarcity of food as the possible reasons. The idea that the male zombie creature could have been functioning in the best interest of the female zombie creature, or with positive intentions was not something that Neville could or would even consider. In fact, his statement that "typical human behavior is now entirely absent" comes directly after him pointing out the peculiar action of the male zombie creature voluntarily exposing himself to the light. As the Zombies are his enemies, and not like him and he not like them, for Neville they could not possibly have good intentions or be doing something grounded in humanity. The intentions of the zombie male must have been self-serving, or driven by something other than nobility. Otherwise, it may have still been showing noble human behavior, and the dehumanized cannot act nobly, because this would humanize them and change how they can be treated.

Neville's choice to attribute the male zombie's actions to things other than good intentions and basic humanity offer insight into how DOD influences an individual's ability to understand those in the out-group who are dissenting. The scene shows how the dehumanizing of an individual prevents a person from seeing nobility in the dehumanized individual's intentions. Even though it is obvious to the viewer that the male zombie creature was willing to risk his own life out of concern for the female zombie character, Neville's polarized view of the creatures prevented him from seeing a similarity in intent and emotions between him and the male zombie creature. He could not, or would not, even consider that the male zombie creature had noble intentions. This is the obscuring of nobility in intentions that comes from polarization. When a group is dehumanized and polarized, to believe they have positive intentions is harder to fathom. That would make them like you and since they can't be like you or you would have to be like them, they can't have intentions similar to yours. Instead, their intentions must be deceitful or malicious.

We can actually see this play out quite often in the realm politics.

Recently the Republican governor of my state cut a significant amount of money from numerous programs in the state budget. The governor's rationale was that he wanted to balance the budget and use the funds for other beneficial programs in the state. This in itself is not abnormal, what was interesting though was the reactions I saw from democratic officials in my state and democratic co-workers at my job (I'm an independent by the way, all this talk of politics I thought you'd want to know). One of my democratic co-workers (we'll call him William), when discussing the cuts stated that the governor only made those cuts to line his own pockets. William believed that the governor's cuts somehow benefitted an organization the Governor was a member of, and that is why he made the cuts. This statement was made in the presence of several other democratic leaning co-workers who promptly jumped in and agreed that the governor was just trying to get rich off his budget allocations. Concurrently I was watching the response to the cuts by many of the democratic elected officials in my state. One of the recurring themes that these democratic officials kept stating was that the governor made the cuts because he doesn't care about the poor or middle class, only about helping his rich friends get richer. This response was especially interesting to me because as elected officials themselves, I would expect them to give other elected officials the benefit of the doubt. I would assume that they would think the governor got into public office for the same reasons many of them did, to help others, not hurt them. Granted some of this is probably political posturing, but I think this same posturing could be done without creating malicious intentions for the governor. In fact in both the case of my co-workers and the case of the democratic elected officials, neither group seem to suggest that the governor had good intentions but was going about it the wrong way. Instead, the out-group nature of the governor and the dehumanization of the out-group obscured this as a possibility. The governor is in a bad out-group thus his intentions must be bad. To be fair I also objected strongly to the cuts by the governor, but I did not feel that he was making them out of malicious intent. Arrogance, maybe, ignorance, probably, but with evil intentions probably not. This story demonstrates the obscuring of nobility and attributing of maliciousness to the intentions of the out-group that result from dehumanization and polarization.

This same obscuring of intentions is not just at play in the political sphere either but it also happens in everyday interactions and situations. I was once told by a supervisor (we'll call her Sally) about an employee (we'll call her Barb) who had obviously embraced the Hater Mindset in her life. This was evident in the responses Barb had when facing dissent. Sally however, was most troubled by a recent situation that had occurred with Barb. When Barb first entered into her position Sally told Barb that Sally saw her ultimate goal as a supervisor being to help Barb develop into the best professional she could be. For more than a year Sally encouraged Barb to take ownership of new tasks, helped find and fund professional development for Barb, encouraged Barb to join larger taskforces and committees for the exposure and knowledge that could be gained from those groups and more. However, on one particular occasion Barb had to be corrected and redirected three different times in a week. Sally believed at this point in their relationship her intentions to help Barb develop and succeed were clear. Any correction or redirection was ultimately to this end. So Sally was completely caught off guard when she was informed that Barb had reported a clashing and contentious work relationship. Sally was informed that

Barb believed Sally was jealous about how great a performer Barb was and was criticizing Barb's performance for that reason. Barb didn't consider that the motivation for the criticism was noble and for her benefit. Instead, she immediately attributed maliciousness to the actions of Sally. Sally's dissent put her in the out-group and thus Barb could not see Sally's positive intentions.

However, it is not just intentions that hinders the opportunity for empathy with out-groups. It is also communication. The refusal by Neville to even consider noble human behavior by the zombie like creature is compounded by the attempt of the male zombie creature to communicate with Neville. In the film, the male zombie character yells at the Neville character after the female zombie character was trapped. This scene is gripping because Neville stares at the creature during its frustration but eventually still concludes that there was no human behavior remaining in the creature. Even though the creature was trying to do one of the things most basic to humanity, communicate. When the zombie creature attempts to communicate with Neville, all Neville hears is a monstrous yell. An uninterpretable sound. Neville could not even fathom the ideas the zombie creature was trying to convey because to Neville these ideas were in a language foreign to him. A language that may not even be human let alone rational.

It is important to note though, that the zombie was indeed communicating. It was actually Neville's inability to be able to understand the zombie's communication that lead to Neville's conclusion that the creatures were devoid of humanity. The issue was Neville's perception not the zombie's communication. As the movie watcher sitting outside of the in-group/out-group enemy situation, the message conveyed by the zombie was clear. We the audience who can still see the humanity in the creatures were able to perceive that the male zombie was upset

179

about someone significant to him being taken. It was Neville's dehumanizing of the zombies that prevented him from understanding the communication of the male zombie. This is the second hindrance to empathy for out-groups caused by dehumanization, the inability to understand their communication.

Almost every depiction of dehumanization results in the inability of the dehumanized being to communicate in the language of the humans. Those who interact with dehumanized individuals in film and fantasy do not interact with them on a shared language level. To the human the dehumanized individual is not smart enough or cognizant enough to speak the language of the human. They are thought to be either too dumb, too ignorant, or to lack the capability to even communicate issues on a basic level. Their points are essentially like a monstrous yell to the member who has dehumanized them. And this is also how the hater mindset views communication from dissenters. This may seem like an outrageous statement at first, but one Sunday morning of political commentary and debate can show how this fact is actually being played out in the culture.

Recently I was watching a political show where two individuals were debating taxes and the economy (we'll call them Tristan and Liam). In the debate, Tristan was arguing for tax cuts for corporations and Liam was arguing for taxes on corporations. During the show something interesting happened. In response to Liam making a point about taxes on corporations being needed Tristan referred to Liam as "a hater". As the conversation continued, the two sides began to share stats and figures to support their argument, then at one point Tristian who had called Liam a "hater" made this statement:

> "those stats don't work, because you don't understand how the economy works. Increasing

money for corporations means more jobs and more money for working people".

Tristan went on to say that what was wrong with Liam's party, is that "they don't understand how the world works. They quote all these stats but they don't have anything to do with how the world and economies actually work". This statement is notable because what Tristan is essentially saying is that Liam doesn't even speak his language. He is arguing that Liam's points are based on ignorant or dumb information. That Liam is in essence not communicating on his level, but is communicating on a level of lower understanding. Just like Neville in the scene with the male zombie, Tristan believed that Liam could not communicate on his level. His words might as well have been a monstrous yell.

And again it's not just politics, similar situations can be seen all the time in contemporary society as well. I often watch individuals in the midst of debates say something along the lines of, "blah, blah, blah. That's all I hear. You just hating. Blah, blah, blah". The individuals in these conversations are quite literally saying, "I can't understand what you're saying. Your words are like gibberish (which is what blah, blah, blah implies). You are speaking at a level too low for me to even comprehend it, let alone care about it. They are implying that the point of the other person is either too dumb, too ignorant, or the person lacks the capacity and capability to communicate with them on their level. Just like Neville, they can't even understand the counterpoints of those that they have dehumanized.

The psychologist Jonathan Haidt in this book *The Righteous Mind: Why Good People are Divided by Politics and Religion*[3] uses a similar example that illustrates the role of dehumanization and polarization in understanding the communication of others. Haidt argues that some individuals, those who classify themselves as liberals, view morality through the lenses of care/harm and fairness. If something is caring, meaning that it does the opposite of harm, and fair and just, than it is moral and right. These are the criteria that define morally right behavior for liberals, fairness and care. Haidt also argues that other individuals, those who classify themselves as conservatives, pull from a larger set of moral foundations. These include care/harm and fairness, but also include loyalty, authority, and sanctity. Haidt makes the point that those individuals who make their moral decisions primarily from care/harm and fairness often cannot understand the counterpoints and conclusions of those individuals who pull their morality from loyalty, authority, and sanctity. Because their lens for morality is through care/harm and fairness, other moral decisions appear foreign to them. Almost as if they are in a different language. Even when others are trying to communicate how they formulated their decisions on morality, the approach is so different that the person whose views are built on care/harm and fairness alone may only hear monstrous yells.

The obscuring of nobility and attributing of maliciousness to the motivations of out-group members, and the difficulty of understanding the communication of out-group members, limits the ability of individuals to empathize with those in their out-group. If an individual believes a person to have malicious intent and cannot understand how they came to their conclusions they will typically assume the worse of that individual. This makes empathy difficult. Empathy is defined as the ability to understand and share the feelings of another. Attribution theory in psychology points out that regardless of what intentions we attribute to others, we almost always attribute positive intentions to ourselves. Meaning that for us, our own intentions are always noble. Thus if we view the intentions of others as malicious it is harder for us to share in the feelings of those others because we will see their intentions as disconnected from ours. Similarly, if we believe the rationale and communication of others to be based on ignorance or dumbness than it becomes harder to truly understand their perspective as well. There point will not seem valid because we can't understand the language and perspective they used to explain it. It will sound like a monstrous yell. In both cases empathy with the out-group becomes harder and harder.

I Only Need You Until I Don't

And while polarization and the encumbering of empathy for others are not healthy elements to have as part of the culture, the third outcome of dehumanization is actually far worse. It is worse because it shapes the way individuals treat those whom they have dehumanized because of dissent. It goes beyond how they view or see the dissenter and guides how they interact with or treat them. The third outcome of dehumanization is that it eliminates the need and desire for bridging capital. It causes people to *use* others who differ from them rather than seek to build connections with them.

Now I know when I said bridging capital some of you immediately thought this book had taken a weird turn into finance (why are we talking about capital?). In truth this line of reasoning is not far off. The term bridging capital is taken from Social Capital Theory, or the theory that each one of an individual's relationship has a sense of value or capital attributed to it. Some relationships have lots of capital, like relationships with friends, family, or spouses. While others have less capital like co-workers, acquaintances, and even strangers. Social Capital Theory argues that there are two types of social capital, bonding capital and bridging capital. Bonding capital is value that is attributed to a relationship because of similarities. Your family and you have similar upbringings, socioeconomic backgrounds, ideologies and more. Thus, you all most likely value each other's relationships because of your similarities. You have bonding capital. Contrastingly bridging capital is value that is attributed to a relationship that is characterized by difference. And it is the type of capital that is needed to bridge dissent. Bridging capital focuses on building norms of reciprocity or mutually beneficial relationships. Relationships where both groups want to see the other benefit as part of their connection or relationship. However, norms of reciprocity or mutually beneficial relationships are not characteristic of dehumanized relationships.

The reason for this is that when a group is dehumanized the person who has dehumanized them does not believe they can benefit from that group. Since the group has negative intentions and their logic is either dumb or ignorant, they offer little in terms of benefit to the person who views them this way. Thus, there becomes little reason to interact with them, except to use them for personal benefit. This is what was seen in the case of Robert Neville in the film I AM LEGEND. Neville saw no reason that he could benefit from the zombie like creatures. They were too dumb, and too much of his enemy to help him. So instead, he used them for the sole purpose of furthering his research. In other words for his own benefit.

As an aside I think it is germane to our topic that for Neville the ultimate point of his research was to make the zombie creatures like him, which would of course make them right again. If they could just be like him everything would be fine. But, while this was Neville's goal it wasn't necessarily the zombie creatures. In the alternate ending it becomes clear that the zombie creatures are not devoid of all logic or rational thought. In

184

the final scene they are able to not only see but to understand that Neville has "cured" one of the female zombie creatures. The creatures choose in this scene not to harm Neville and to pay special attention to the captured female zombie creature. Yet upon seeing the "cured" female the other zombies do not stay around to be "cured" by Neville. They instead take the female creature and leave, as if content to have gotten their female counterpart back. The scene is a wonderful illustration of the two vantage points on dehumanization. One side is doing everything they can to convert the other side, because that would make them right. Make them human. Meanwhile the other side has little interest in converting because they don't view themselves as wrong.

Neville's interaction of using the dehumanized zombies for his benefit is also a great parallel for how the Hater Mindset and its DOD causes individuals to view dissenters as things to be used rather than people with which to build relationships. As an example when I was researching this book one of the most popular memes I ran across were ones that had a similar theme to the statement "I keep my haters around because they help me to push myself harder". The idea here is that the hater adds no value to the individual's life except to help them do better themselves. The hater's role is to benefit the person they are "hating on". There is no respect for the perspective of the hater, no discussion of how the hater's views force dialogue so that both sides grow. There is no desire to see the "hater" benefit at all. Just an emphasis on how haters can be used for self -benefit. This meme idea is constantly seen in everyday interactions as well. People believe that those who dissent from them should only be used to benefit from, not to build a mutually beneficial relationship with. This was perfectly illustrated to me in one of the stories that began this book. My niece was glad to use me to help her ride her bike, but in the moment where she felt I dissented from her, I no longer needed to benefit from civility or politeness, I only needed to make sure that she learned to ride a bike. Anything outside of that was not needed. It was hating. The dissent caused her to see me as a resource to be used not a person to be valued. This is the approach people take to dissent in contemporary culture. Since they don't see a reason to engage with the dissenter, they would rather avoid them (see chapter 4), unless of course they can benefit from them. And this causes people to not seek bridging capital, but instead they seek to use those who dissent from them.

Summary

The conservative scholar Paul Gottfried coined the term the dehumanization of dissent as a way to describe how individuals in society were handling dissenting views. This chapter examined how dehumanization affects the way we view, interact, communicate, and treat others who dissent. The notion of dehumanization is the idea that when a person dissents or differs they are not like the person from whom they are dissenting. They are somehow disconnected from them, and the human value and decency, associated with them. This view of individuals as disconnected from the humanity of others leads to a view of them as enemies and eventually to polarization. Polarization then makes it difficult for individuals to ascribe nobility to the intentions of others, and for them to understand the rationale and language that those who dissent from them use to explain their perspective. This ultimately causes individuals to lose the desire and need for bridging capital with these individuals. Instead, it becomes much easier to simply use them for personal benefit. This is the outcome of the "just a" in the "you are just a hater sentence". It causes those who have embraced the Hater Mindset to devalue relationships and ultimately to polarize, lose empathy for, and use others for personal benefit.

PART 5 – HATER REVISITED

Chapter 10 – BE A HATER

I'm A Hater. Don't Like it? Good
-   Grumpy Cat Meme

When I was growing up I used to love to listen to music, but not just for the enjoyment of it. As a conceptual thinker, I loved to listen to each song looking for the overall connective themes or ideas that inspired the artist to create and title their album whatever it was titled. I liked to believe there was an overall structure to how everything was put together. Occasionally, I would listen to an album that would do something that irked me to the core. That thing that irked me, was the end of the album title song. For those of you not familiar with this concept, when albums are titled there is often a song on the album that holds the same title as the album itself. This is called the title track or title song of the album. If the album was called *All Eyez on Me*, there would be a track on the album called All Eyez on Me (phenomenal album by the way). Similarly, if the album was called Piano Man there would be a song on the album called Piano Man. Being that the title track is the same as the title of the album the listener can expect that the title track covers some of the major themes the artists engaged with during the creation of the album. Or even better, it outlines several of the concepts that will be covered throughout the album's other songs. Some artist when having a title track were kind enough to put it early in the album. The first track on the album "Straight of Compton" is titled … you guessed it "Straight Out of Compton". However, other artists for some reason would not provide this easy access to the title track. They would instead make the last track of the album the title track. I would have to listen to all of the other tracks on the album before reaching the track that sparked the name of the album (or vice versa). This always struck me as odd thing to do and often bothered me. Why wait until the end of the album to share the track that everyone naturally expects to be on the album? It made no sense to me. Which is why I find it ironic that when I had the chance to produce my own creative work (this book) I find myself utilizing the same approach that frustrated me all those years ago. I have put the title chapter of the book at the end. The name of this book is called "BE A HATER: A Polemic on the Hater Mindset". A reader would naturally expect to see a chapter in this book called "Be A Hater". Yet instead of placing this chapter first and foremost in the book making for easy access, I have placed the chapter at the end of the book the same way that musicians place their title tracks at the end of the album. But by placing it here, I not only mimic the albums that used to irk me, I also finally understand the mindset of all the musical artist that I misunderstood for so long. I understand why a song that covers many of the themes that may be shared throughout the rest of the album or the title chapter of a book is placed at the end. The reason why is that these songs or chapters do not serve as an introduction to the themes present in the album or book or even as a summary of them. They in fact, as this chapter does, serve as a response to those ideas and concepts. The title chapter or title track may not be designed to introduce a set of ideas, but as a way to resolve them, or at the very least respond to them. This is where the final chapter of this book finds itself. Not as an introduction, a summary, or even a recap of ideas shared earlier, but as a response to them.

I began this book by stating that I am vehemently, passionately, and unashamedly a hater, and that my ultimate goal was to convince you the reader to join me and become an unapologetic hater as well. I argued that in order to do this I would have to define what meaning I am imbuing into the term hater and why I think it is a better alternative to what I am calling the "Hater Mindset". I then used the next several chapters to explain what meaning society imbues into the term hater and how it leads to the Hater Mindset. I laid out the damage and dangers of the Hater Mindset as a phenomenon embedded in culture and society. And by utilizing this approach I was actually able to do two things. The first is that I was able to expose the hidden and subconscious themes of the Hater Mindset making them more visible for individuals in society, culture, and organizations, to be able to counter and address them. The second is that by approaching the structure of the book this way I have also created a scaffold on which to bridge into my definition of what it means to be a hater. I have laid the foundation on which my definition of a hater can be juxtaposed against. Thereby stating not just what you accomplish by being a hater but also what you avoid. Throughout this book I have argued that society presents the view of a hater as someone

> **who holds a position, opinion, view, or perspective that is different from the position, opinion, view, or perspective that you currently hold.**

And I claimed that this view leads to a mindset and approach to dissent that is dangerous. One that I title the Hater Mindset and define as

> **the mindset that labels others a hater due to their dissenting views and predisposes individuals to lower levels of critical thinking, innovation, tolerance of dissent, and epistemic motivation. While also fostering a mindset of entitlement, and a devaluing of relationships.**

193

I now turn to conceptualizing the idea of a hater revised as scaffolded against these two definitions. Not as a concept separate in itself but as one juxtaposed against the information presented earlier in this book. And since the other elements of this book are outlined based on the sentence "you are just a hater", it seems only fitting that my conception of a hater in this chapter is outlined using a counter sentence. And what better counter to the sentence, "you are just a hater" than the sentence, "I am a hater".

Not only does the statement "I am a hater" appear at face value to be the opposite to the sentence "You are just a hater", the response on the face of others when I reply, "I am a hater" after being called one is priceless. However, it is the feeling that is evoked through the sentence that makes it useful as the outline for my conception of a hater. That feeling is normally "curiosity". The shock or surprise on the face of individuals when I say, "I am a hater" is actually masked curiosity. They want to know why I would say that. Who admits to being a hater? Does he know what a hater is? And other similar questions. It creates what was described earlier as an information gap and a way to produce learning. "I am just a hater" as a response increases epistemic curiosity and encourages investigation. And in the nature of this investigation, I begin my examination of the "I am a hater" sentence at the opposite end of where I began the "you are just a hater" examination, at the beginning with the word "I".

"I"

The word "I" is especially fitting as the beginning of the "I am a hater" sentence because it is the opposite of the word "you" which is the first word in the "you are just a hater" sentence. It is not opposite merely in the personal pronoun sense, but opposite in the very nature of the word. Earlier in this book, I argued that the "you" in the "you are just a hater" sentence represented a projection. The word "you" allowed the speaker to project their fear of being wrong on to the person with which they are speaking. This projection lead to cognitive entitlement and guiltlessness both of which I argued are not elements that lead to stronger societies or cultures. However, while "you" may point to projection, the word "I" does just the opposite. Intrinsic to the word "I" is the idea of introspection. Whenever a person uses the word "I", they are naturally reflecting on themselves. It is impossible to begin a sentence with the word "I" without making some sort of self-reflective observation. So immediately, the sentence "I am a hater" distinguishes itself from the "you are just a hater" sentence by having a focus on introspection instead projection. This is the first precept for my definition of a hater revised. If society's conception of a hater focuses on projection, my conception of a hater revised is one that focuses on introspection. And if projection leads to cognitive entitlement, declining metacognition, and guiltlessness, introspection does the opposite. Introspection has been shown to have numerous benefits for individuals. It increases the likelihood and effectiveness of metacognition, which as was discussed earlier has been linked to critical thinking, innovation, personal growth, and more. When an individual practices introspection as a response to dissent they are able to think more thoroughly about why they concluded what they thought, how that process came about, and what those ideas should be measured against. These contemplations lead to better evaluation of whether those thoughts are right or wrong and increases the likelihood of guilt, which decreases the potential for guiltlessness and cognitive entitlement. But introspection can also lead to more basic things like tact, eloquence, and humility.

When I refer to tact here, I am referring to the ability to know when and what to say at the right time. Dictionary.com defines it as "a keen sense of what to say or do to avoid giving offense". Tact is a great skill to acquire because it helps people to navigate difficult decisions, especially during dissent. A person who practices introspection in response to dissent is more likely to thoroughly evaluate their own ideas, to measure their responses, and to be able to explain their point more comprehensively. This leads to tact as the individual measures when and how to deliver their responses, so that they are more thoughtful and targeted before saying them.

Introspection also leads to eloquence. A person who practices introspection as a response to dissent cogitates more deeply on their thoughts and perspective. Thus, they are more likely to be able to explain their point of view completely, succinctly, and clearly. My undergraduate degree is in communications and one of the first points taught during this degree is that the better and more thoroughly you understand your topic the easier it is for you to articulate it. Similarly, I once had a mentor who said if your thoughts on a subject are not at least three questions deep (meaning that you should be able to answer at least three questions someone asked about whatever topic you are discussing) than you have not thought enough on the topic. Introspection leads to a three question deep understanding of a topic. It causes an individual to think through their points and also forces them to formulate internal language during this thought process. Individuals think in both concepts and in language. They are constantly converting mental concepts into internal language. This is why we often have an idea that we can't put the words to. Our brains have the concept but it is working on forming language to

196

explain it to ourselves. Thus having formulated or at least attempted to formulate internal language, and having thought thoroughly through their points the individual who practices introspection is more likely to be able to share their ideas completely ,succinctly, clearly, and eloquently.

Introspection in response to dissent can also lead to humility as well. An individual who introspects in response to dissent may determine from their introspection that they are wrong. As was discussed earlier people typically exist in a state of error blindness. We are aware that we may be wrong but we are unaware where we are wrong. In order to determine if we are wrong we have to be able to introspect. The individual who introspects evaluates their own thoughts and considers that they may be in error. Thus, this individual may be less likely to feel entitled to their view or to affirm their own rightness in each situation without proper evaluation. They may be less inclined to be prideful in their perspective and thoughts, and more inclined to take a humble approach to new information. This response to dissent and possible wrongness I would argue is a much more productive and beneficial approach than projection. And humility is arguably a better way to go through life in general. One reason for this was provided by Jim Collins in his discussion of LEVEL 5 leaders, or the highest level of leadership. Collins argues that personal humility is key to LEVEL 5 leaders.[1] It helps them to be aware of their possible blind spots and errors and pulls out the best in their followers. The Level 5 leader doesn't shut down dissent but embraces it with humility because it leads to innovation, problem solving, and growth. I would argue that Level 5 leaders are the type of leaders that would be strong additions to culture and society. And that means introspection and humility.

My challenge to culture and society to "BE A

HATER" begins by encouraging us as individuals to move past projection in response to dissent, to move to introspection. I challenge us to use introspection to gain critical thinking, tact, humility, and more. Instead of falling prey to guiltlessness, cognitive entitlement, and malleable ethics. To respond to dissent with "I" instead of "you". This is the first precept of being a hater revised.

"Am A"

The second precept of my conception of a hater revised is found through the examination of the "am a" in the sentence "I am a hater". The words "am a" in this sentence are notable not just for what they do say but for what they don't. They are notable for what is absent. The words "am a" in the "I am a hater" sentence are present without the word "just". As discussed earlier the word "just" is easy to skip over in sentences but its presence actually adds significant meaning to a sentence or phrase. The word "just" denotes a lack of uniqueness and a lack of value. This was discussed earlier in chapter 8. The word "just" if added to the "I am a hater" sentence would change the sentence dramatically. Stripping it of any implied meanings of value and uniqueness. "I am just a hater", signifies both a lack of value and a lack of uniqueness. However, the absence of the word "just" adds at least one of these things, if not both, back into the sentence. Its absence definitely signals uniqueness. And I would argue that in most cases the absence of "just" signals value as well.

Think about the phrase "am a". It is almost impossible to imagine a scenario where "am a" is not following the word "I". The person who says "I am a" is declaring themselves to be part of a group. The idea of being "a" indicates that there are others who are like them in this category and others who are not like them in this category. It creates a group. A group with a membership criterion that not everyone fits. The word "a" implies there are others who *are* also whatever you are saying you *are*. But, by nature there are others who *are not* what you say you are. And in most cases the person saying "I am a" is declaring themselves to be a member of a group that they value. "I am a Patriots fan" or "I am a stud". In these cases, the individual is not only conveying connection to a group but value for the group with which they are aligning themselves.

This again stands in contrast to the Hater Mindset and the contemporary understanding of a hater. In the "you are just a hater" approach to dissent an individual responds to dissent by distancing themselves from the person they are dubbing a hater. They seek to dehumanize and disconnect from the person dissenting. To disassociate from them. This is different from my conception of a hater revised. While the Hater Mindset wants to distance itself from dissenters, diminishing them as common, not unique, and not valuable, my conception of a hater revised takes the opposite approach. It starts with affirming value and uniqueness for the relationships that an individual currently has. It focuses on the memberships and shared experience that the individual has with others. "I am a" affirms membership in a group and value for that group. It affirms relationships not devalues them.

Notice also, that the "I am a hater" sentence does not diminish, attack, or even criticize the other person or their associated groups. It only affirms the value and membership an individual has for their own group. It focuses on unique value being brought to the discussion, not dissenting perspective being pushed away. The person who embraces the "I am a hater" approach recognizes that relationships are unique and valuable. But not just any relationships, relationships that differ from

199

the person they are talking to. The "I am a hater" approach leaves the door open for bridging capital. The person who uses this approach is in essence saying, my group and I's perspective has value to you. "I am a republican" or "I am a democrat" asserts that my view has value for other political thinkers. "Am a" focuses on value being brought by my group and I to the other group or person. And by reciprocity, their view has value to me. This conception of a hater revised recognizes that dissenting ideas lead to better performance, that diverse perspectives sharpen thinking and decision making, that differing views force people to search for common ground (build bridging capital) in order to work together. It fosters critical thinking by allowing for diverse ideas and views to be shared and evaluated. And it does all this without diminishing those who hold different views.

In short the "am a" in the "I am a hater" sentence offers two elements that distinguish my conception of a hater revised from the hater and Hater Mindset discussed earlier in this book. The "am a" signals a value for relationships. Valuing them as unique and important. But not only valuing relationships with the in-group, valuing relationships with members of out-groups as well. Seeing them as assets who help make better decisions, produce innovation, and spark individual growth, rather than viewing them as enemies to be polarized against. Thus, the second precept of my hater revised conception and challenge to be a hater is for us as individuals to value relationships in general as special and unique, and to seek out relationships with those who may differ from us. Those who may be in our out-group. Not for the purpose of diminishing them, or converting them, but so that we can learn and grow from them. This I argue is what it would truly mean to be a hater.

"Hater"

When I began the evaluation of the Hater Mindset earlier in this book I thought it best to provide an examination of the word "hater" before the other words in the "you are just a hater" sentence. I proposed that "hater" represented the piece de resistance of the "you are just a hater" sentence and that without placing it into proper context an evaluation of the other parts of the sentence would lack conceptual meaning and depth. It is only fitting then that in my response to the Hater Mindset that my examination of the word "hater" be completed last. For just like in the examination of the Hater Mindset and the "you are just a hater" sentence we find the word "hater" at the core of the "I am a hater" message as well. And while the Hater Mindset caused me to evaluate the sentence starting backwards (symbolizing a backwards thinking about dissent) I propose that my conception of hater corrects wrong thinking and thus I can evaluate the "I am a hater" sentence in proper order with "hater" last (I know that was a lot of symbolism, but stick with me).

So what then is my conception of a "hater" and what meaning am I imbuing into the word "hater"? To answer these questions we once again turn to a scaffolded understanding of the term hater. I wrote earlier that when someone calls someone else a "hater" what they are really referring to is that person's dissent. I used the work of Cass Sunstein on dissent to outline two types of dissent disclosing dissent and contrarian dissent. Contrarian dissent is dissent that exists for the sole purpose of disagreeing. It is not about offering new information or adding new perspective to the current group, it is about disagreeing for the sake of disagreeing[2]. This type of dissent while still having some benefit can often lead to strife and frustration. On the other hand disclosing dissent is quite beneficial. It has been shown to add new perspectives and information to a group. To improve decision-making and decision-making processes. And to encourage critical thinking, by forcing others to evaluate new information in light of the information they currently hold. I argued that the contemporary definition of a "hater" depicted the "hater" as a contrarian and this caused individuals to not be interested, to not listen, and to not direct their attention to the dissent they face. This in turn limited the critical thinking, the exposure, the learning, and the growth of individuals. My conception of a hater revised challenges individuals to not view dissent as contrarian but to view it as disclosing.

This is the third precept of being a hater. The hater as I have conceptualized it views dissent differently than contemporary culture. It views dissent as disclosing. Instead of avoiding the cognitive dissonance that could come from new information, it embraces it. The new view of a "hater" is aware of and constantly monitoring cognitive dissonance. For this type of "hater" dissonance doesn't occur only at the subconscious or implicit level. Introspection driven by the "I" pushes this dissonance to the conscious mind where it can be evaluated. Where it is greeted with excitement as an opportunity to rethink a perspective, or to learn something new.

The view of dissent and dissonance as opportunities for thought causes my conception of a hater revised to practice critical thinking often. They view dissent as a way to implement Brookfield's critical thinking steps. As a way to evaluate their own thoughts, and then as a way to evaluate them against the perspectives and ideas of others. For them this is invigorating not frustrating.

This conception of a hater applies cognitive effort toward dissent. They do not believe they are entitled to their thinking. As individuals they are interested in, listening to, and applying their attention toward information that differs from their own cognitive ideas. For them dissent is a way to increase their epistemic motivation by intentionally producing information gaps. To stay curious. To learn. To improve.

A "hater revised" as I conceptualize it also sees wrongness differently than the contemporary version of a hater. The person who affirms, "I am a hater" considers the idea that they may be wrong. They understand that they may be on the wrong side of whatever is being decided. And this is not scary to them. They believe like the theologian Alexander Pope that to err is to be human[3]. It is okay to err as this allows us to learn.

Since each of the precepts of my conception of a hater revised are juxtaposed against the concepts that make up the Hater Mindset it would make sense that a formalized definition of my conception of hater would simply be the opposite of the formalized definition of the Hater Mindset. In chapter 1 of this book I proposed that the Hater Mindset could be defined as

> **the mindset that labels others a hater due to their dissenting views and predisposes individuals to lower levels of critical thinking, while also fostering a mindset of entitlement, and a devaluing of relationships.**

And this definition was based on the contemporary understanding of a hater as :

> **A person who holds a position, opinion, view, or perspective that is different from the position, opinion, view, or perspective that you currently hold.**

Throughout this book I sought to explain why both of these definitions are problematic for the current culture, and how a better understanding of the concept of a hater is needed. And so at the end of this book, I once again reiterate my definition of a hater revised as:

A person who actively combats the Hater Mindset, by pursuing dissent, doubting their own presuppositions, and applying value to existing relationships even in the midst of disagreement.

And I challenge you the reader to join me in redefining and re-conceptualizing the idea of a hater. Moving away from a mindset that devalues relationships, limits critical thinking, produces cognitive entitlement and damages our society, our world, and our culture. And embracing a definition that engages introspection instead of projection, that values relationships with those like us and those unlike us, and views dissent as disclosing instead of contrarian. In short, one that will help build stronger individuals, a stronger society, and a stronger culture. So here at the end of this book, I revisit the request that I made in chapter 1. I have decided that I am vehemently, passionately, and unashamedly A HATER!!! And my hope is that here at the end of this book you join me and declare yourself to be an unapologetic hater as well. Will you join me and BE A HATER?!

NOTES

CHAPTER 2

[1] Swift, T. (2014) Lyrics from Taylor Swifts "Shake it Off" song on the Album 1989

[2] Rainer, T. S., & Rainer, J. W. (2011). *The millennials: connecting to America's largest generation.* Nashville, TN.B&H Publishing Group.

[3] Twenge, J. M. (2014). *Generation me-revised and updated: Why today's young Americans are more confident, assertive, entitled--and more miserable than ever before.* New York, NY: Simon and Schuster.

[4] Rainer, T. S., & Rainer, J. W. (2011). *The millennials: connecting to America's largest generation.* Nashville, TN.B&H Publishing Group.

[5] Rainer, T. S., & Rainer, J. W. (2011). *The millennials: connecting to America's largest generation.* Nashville, TN.B&H Publishing Group. p.2-3.

[6] Rainer, T. S., & Rainer, J. W. (2011). *The millennials: connecting to America's largest generation.* Nashville, TN.B&H Publishing Group.

[7] Lorenz, T. (2017, July 16) Forget about Millennials-experts are now going after marketing to Generation Z. Retrieved from http://www.businessinsider.com/experts-are-marketing-to-generation-z-2017-7

[8] Kohut, A., Parker, K., Keeter, S., Doherty, C., & Dimock, M. (2007, January 9).*A portrait of "Generation Next": How young people view their lives, futures and politics.* Pew Research Center. Available On-line: http://peoplepress.org/reports/display.php3?ReportID=300"

[9] Deal, J. J., Altman, D. G., & Rogelberg, S. G. (2010). Millennials at work: What we know and what we need to do (if anything). *Journal of Business and Psychology, 25*(2), 191-199.

[10] Rainer, T. S., & Rainer, J. W. (2011). *The millennials: connecting to America's largest generation.* B&H Publishing Group.

[11] Campbell, W. K., Hoffman, B. J., Campbell, S. M., & Marchisio, G. (2011). Narcissism in organizational contexts. *Human Resource Management Review, 21*(4), 268-284.

[12] Rainer, T. S., & Rainer, J. W. (2011). *The millennials: connecting to America's largest generation.* B&H Publishing Group. p.2.

[13] Schein, E. (2010), *Organizational Culture and Leadership*, John Wiley and Sons Inc., San Francisco, CA. p.18

[14] This information was found at Un.org

[15] Merriam, A. P., & Merriam, V. (1964). *The anthropology of music*. Evanston, IL: Northwestern University Press. P.223

[16] Cassano, M. E., & ACHt, R. (2005). Hypnosis and 'Heavy Metal'· Musical Modalities for Treating Trauma. *Journal of Heart-Centered Therapies, 8*(2), 41-61.

[17] Kajikawa, L. (2014). Hip Hop History in the Age of Colorblindness. *Journal of Music History Pedagogy, 5*(1), 117-23.

[18] Zickuhr, K. (2011, February 3) Generations and their Gadgets. Retrieved from http://www.pewinternet.org/2011/02/03/generations-and-their-gadgets/

[19] Resnikoff, P.(2016, June 2) Millennials listen to 75% more music than baby Boomers, Study finds. Retrieved from https://www.digitalmusicnews.com/2016/06/02/millennials-listen-more-music-baby-boomers/ Note: A second report by BPI and ERA confirmed this data in 2017. This report can be found here http://eraltd.org/media/27138/midia-research-gen-z-report.pdf

[20] This information was drawn from a report by trifecta research. The report was titled Generation Z Meida Consumption Habits and can be retrieved here: http://trifectaresearch.com/wp-content/uploads/2015/09/Generation-Z-Sample-Trifecta-Research-Deliverable.pdf

[21] Boroditsky, L. (2011). How language shapes thought. *Scientific American*, *304*(2), 62-65.

[22] Ostrom, V. (1976). The contemporary debate over centralization and decentralization. *Publius*, *6*(4), 21-32.

[23] Fuks, A. (2011). Healing, wounding, and the language of medicine. In *Whole Person Care* (pp. 83-95). Springer New York. p.83.

[24] Beckner, C., Blythe, R., Bybee, J., Christiansen, M. H., Croft, W., Ellis, N. C., Holland, J., Ke, Jy., Larsen-Freeman, D.,Schoenemann, T. (2009). Language is a complex adaptive system: Position paper. *Language learning*, *59*(s1), 1-26.

[25] Beckner, C., Blythe, R., Bybee, J., Christiansen, M. H., Croft, W., Ellis, N. C., Holland, J., Ke, Jy., Larsen-Freeman, D.,Schoenemann, T. (2009). Language is a complex adaptive system: Position paper. *Language learning*, *59*(s1),P.9

[26] This information was drawn from a report by trifecta research. The report was titled Generation Z Meida Consumption Habits and can be retrieved here: http://trifectaresearch.com/wp-content/uploads/2015/09/Generation-Z-Sample-Trifecta-Research-Deliverable.pdf

[27] The 2017 BPI and ERA report emphasized music as a way for Generation Z and Millennials to have fun and interact with friends http://eraltd.org/media/27138/midia-research-gen-z-report.pdf

Chapter 3

[1] Kedmey, D. (2014, Oct 15) Toyota Recalls 1.7 Million Vehicles Worldwide over Range of Defects. Retrieved from http://time.com/3510125/toyota-recalls-1-7-million-vehicles-worldwide-over-range-of-defects/

[2] Schulz, Kathryn (2010) Being Wrong: Adventures in the Margin of Error. New York: HarperCollins Books

[3] Schulz, Kathryn (2010) Being Wrong: Adventures in the Margin of Error. New York: HarperCollins Books

[4] Boroditsky, L. (2011). How language shapes thought. *Scientific American*, *304*(2), 62-65.

[5]Payne, R.K. (2005). A framework for understanding poverty (4th ed.). Highlands, TX: Aha! Process, Inc.

[6]Payne, R.K. (2005). A framework for understanding poverty (4th ed.). Highlands, TX: Aha! Process, Inc. p.37

[7] Mackey, R. D. (2015). *Beyond" pushing play": The implications of technology on music composition and performance* (Doctoral dissertation, Wichita State University). P.6
Mackey was referencing the work of Dowling, W. J., & Harwood, D. L. (1986). Music cognition. New York: Academic Press.

[8] Heslet, L. (2003). Our musical brain. *Musica human research*.

[9] Heslet, L. (2003). Our musical brain. *Musica human research*.p.5

[10]Cassano, M. E., & ACHt, R. (2005). Hypnosis and 'Heavy Metal': Musical Modalities for Treating Trauma. *Journal of Heart-Centered Therapies*, *8*(2), p.42.

[11] Donovan, E. (2010). Propranolol use in the prevention and treatment of posttraumatic stress disorder in military veterans: forgetting therapy revisited. *Perspectives in biology and medicine*, *53*(1), p. 67

[12] Donovan, E. (2010). Propranolol use in the prevention and treatment of posttraumatic stress disorder in military veterans: forgetting therapy revisited. *Perspectives in biology and medicine*, *53*(1), 61-74. p.63).

[13] Loftus, E. F., & Palmer, J. C. (1996). Eyewitness testimony. In *Introducing Psychological Research* (pp. 305-309). Macmillan Education UK.

[14] Juslin, P. N., & Sloboda, J. (Eds.). (2011). *Handbook of music and emotion: Theory, research, applications*. Oxford University Press.

[15] Juslin, P. N., & Sloboda, J. (Eds.). (2011). *Handbook of music and emotion: Theory, research, applications*. Oxford University Press.

[16] Cassano, M. E., & ACHt, R. (2005). Hypnosis and 'Heavy Metal': Musical Modalities for Treating Trauma. *Journal of Heart-Centered Therapies*, *8*(2), p.42.

Chapter 4

[1] Definition taken from dictionary. com

[2] Sunstein, C. R. (2005). *Why societies need dissent* (Vol. 9). Cambridge, MA: Harvard University Press.

[3] Sunstein, C. R. (2005). *Why societies need dissent* (Vol. 9). Cambridge, MA: Harvard University Press. p,85

[4] Sunstein, C. R. (2005). *Why societies need dissent* (Vol. 9). Cambridge, MA: Harvard University Press. p,85

[5] Sunstein, C. R. (2005). *Why societies need dissent* (Vol. 9). Cambridge, MA: Harvard University Press. p,1

[6] Sunstein, C. R. (2005). *Why societies need dissent* (Vol. 9). Cambridge, MA: Harvard University Press. p,35

Chapter 5

[1] Dockterman. E. (2014, Aug 19) Taylor Swift's 'Shake it Off' and 7 Other Songs about Haters. Retrieved from http://time.com/3140091/taylor-swifts-shake-it-off-and-7-other-songs-about-haters/

[2] Cooper, J. (2007). *Cognitive dissonance: 50 years of a classic theory*. Sage.

[3] Cooper, J. (2007). *Cognitive dissonance: 50 years of a classic theory*. Sage.p.5

[4] Aronson, E. & Aronson, J. (2008). The social animal (10th ed). New York, NY: Worth Publishers. P. 184

[5] Aronson, E. & Aronson, J. (2008). The social animal (10th ed). New York, NY: Worth Publishers

[6] Hoover, J. D. (2014). Complexity avoidance, narcissism and experiential learning. *Developments in Business Simulation and Experiential Learning, 38*.

[7] McFalls, E. L., & Cobb-Roberts, D. (2001). Reducing resistance to diversity through cognitive dissonance instruction: Implications for teacher education. *Journal of teacher education, 52*(2), 164-172.

[8] Chabrak, N., & Craig, R. (2013). Student imaginings, cognitive dissonance and critical thinking. *Critical Perspectives on Accounting*, *24*(2), 91-104.

[9] Arnold, D. L. (1938). Testing ability to use data in the fifth and sixth grades. *Educational Research Bulletin*, 255-278.

[10] Proftto-McGrath, J. (2003). The relationship of critical thinking skills and critical thinking dispositions of baccalaureate nursing students. *Journal of advanced nursing*, *43*(6), 569-577. (Profetto-McGrath et al, 2003)

[11] Browne, M. N., Freeman, K. E., & Williamson, C. L. (2000). The importance of critical thinking for student use of the Internet. *College Student Journal*, *34*(3), 391-391.

[12] Brookfield, S. D. (2011). *Teaching for critical thinking: Tools and techniques to help students question their assumptions*. John Wiley & Sons.

[13]Brookfield, S. D. (2011). *Teaching for critical thinking: Tools and techniques to help students question their assumptions*. John Wiley & Sons.

[14] Loewenstein, G. (1994). The psychology of curiosity: A review and reinterpretation. *Psychological bulletin*, *116*(1), 75.

[15] Leslie, I. (2014). *Curious: The desire to know and why your future depends on it*. Philadelphia, PA: .Basic Books.

[16] Leslie, I. (2014). *Curious: The desire to know and why your future depends on it*. Philadelphia, PA: Basic Books.

[17] Leslie, I. (2014). *Curious: The desire to know and why your future depends on it*. Philadelphia, PA: Basic Books.p.40

[18] Pariser, E. (2011). *The filter bubble: How the new personalized web is changing what we read and how we think.* New York: Penguin Press

[19] Pariser, E. (2011). *The filter bubble: How the new personalized web is changing what we read and how we think.* New York: Penguin Press

[20] Pariser, E. (2011). *The filter bubble: How the new personalized web is changing what we read and how we think.* New York: Penguin Press

[21] Attention. (2003). In *Merriam-Webster's dictionary* (11th ed.). Springfield, MA:

[22] De Dreu, C. K., Nijstad, B. A., Bechtoldt, M. N., & Baas, M. (2011). Group creativity and innovation: A motivated information processing perspective. *Psychology of Aesthetics, Creativity, and the Arts, 5*(1), p.82

[23] Van Kleef, G. A., Homan, A. C., Beersma, B., Van Knippenberg, D., Van Knippenberg, B., & Damen, F. (2009). Searing sentiment or cold calculation? The effects of leader emotional displays on team performance depend on follower epistemic motivation. *Academy of Management Journal, 52*(3),p. 565)

[24] Schulz, Kathryn (2010) Being Wrong: Adventures in the Margin of Error. New York: HarperCollins Books

CHAPTER 6

[1] Betz, A. (2013). The art and science of effective feedback: What works, what does not… and why. *Human Resource Management International Digest, 21*(2), 37-40.

[2] Description is from Harper-Collins Website https://www.harpercollins.com/9780062012401/being-wrong

[3] Schulz, Kathryn (2010) Being Wrong: Adventures in the Margin of Error. New York: HarperCollins Books. p.4

[4] Schulz, Kathryn (2010) Being Wrong: Adventures in the Margin of Error. New York: HarperCollins Books. p.4

[5] Grubbs, J. B., & Exline, J. J. (2016). Trait entitlement: A cognitive-personality source of vulnerability to psychological distress.

[6] Proust, J. (2013). *The philosophy of metacognition: Mental agency and self-awareness*. OUP Oxford. p. 124

and

Burge, T. (2003). Perceptual entitlement. *Philosophy and phenomenological research*, *67*(3), 503-548.

CHAPTER 7

[1] De Dreu, C. K., Nijstad, B. A., & van Knippenberg, D. (2008). Motivated information processing in group judgment and decision making. *Personality and Social Psychology Review*, *12*(1), 22-49.

[2] Proust, J. (2013). *The philosophy of metacognition: Mental agency and self-awareness*. OUP Oxford.

[3] Proust, J. (2013). *The philosophy of metacognition: Mental agency and self-awareness*. OUP Oxford.

[4] Proust, J. (2008, October). XIII—Epistemic Agency and Metacognition: An Externalist View. In *Proceedings of the Aristotelian Society (Hardback)* (Vol. 108, No. 1pt3, pp. 241-268). Blackwell Publishing Ltd.

[5] Bialik,M. (2015, November 5) Meta-Learning: The importance of Thinking about Thinking. Retrieved from https://www.learningandthebrain.com/blog/meta-learning/

This research was also chronicled by :

Fadel, C., Bialik, M., & Trilling, B. (2015). *Four-dimensional education: The competencies learners need to succeed*. Center for Curriculum Redesign. And

Gourgey,A. "Metacognition in Basic Skills Instruction," Instructional Science 26, no. 1 (1998): 81–96

[6] Palmer, J. S. (2014). The Millennials Are Coming: Improving Self-Efficacy in Law Students through Universal Design in Learning. *Clev. St. L. Rev.*, *63*,

[7] Horney, N., Pasmore, B., & O'Shea, T. (2010). Leadership agility: A business imperative for a VUCA world. *Human Resource Planning*, *33*(4).

[8] Korhonen, J. J., Hiekkanen, K., & Heiskala, M. (2010). Map to Service-Oriented Business and IT: A Stratified Approach. In *AMCIS* (p. 157).p.157.

[9] Hammond, M. M., Neff, N. L., Farr, J. L., Schwall, A. R., & Zhao, X. (2011). Predictors of individual-level innovation at work: A meta-analysis. p.99

[10] Tangney, J. P., Stuewig, J., Mashek, D., & Hastings, M. (2011). Assessing jail inmates' proneness to shame and guilt: Feeling bad about the behavior or the self?. *Criminal justice and behavior*, *38*(7), 715.

[11] Cohen, T. R., Panter, A. T., & Turan, N. (2012). Guilt proneness and moral character. *Current Directions in Psychological Science*, *21*(5), 355-359.

[12] Callahan, D. (2007). *The cheating culture: Why more Americans are doing wrong to get ahead*. Boston, MA. Houghton Mifflin Harcourt.

[13] Callahan, D. (2007). *The cheating culture: Why more Americans are doing wrong to get ahead*. Boston, MA. Houghton Mifflin Harcourt. P.13

[14] [14]Callahan, D. (2007). *The cheating culture: Why more Americans are doing wrong to get ahead.* Boston, MA. Houghton Mifflin Harcourt. P.13

[15] Tangney, J. P., Stuewig, J., Mashek, D., & Hastings, M. (2011). Assessing jail inmates' proneness to shame and guilt: Feeling bad about the behavior or the self?. *Criminal justice and behavior*, *38*(7), 715.

[16] Grubbs, J. B., & Exline, J. J. (2016). Trait entitlement: A cognitive-personality source of vulnerability to psychological distress.

[17] Moeller, S. J., Crocker, J., & Bushman, B. J. (2009). Creating hostility and conflict: Effects of entitlement and self-image goals. *Journal of Experimental Social Psychology*, *45*(2), p. 448

CHAPTER 8

[1] Waldinger, R. (November, 2015). What Makes a Good Life? Lessons from the Longest study on Happiness [Video File]. Retrieved from https://www.ted.com/talks/robert_waldinger_what_makes_a_good_life_lessons_from_the_longest_study_on_happiness

[2] Waldinger, R. (November, 2015). What Makes a Good Life? Lessons from the Longest study on Happiness [Video File]. Retrieved from https://www.ted.com/talks/robert_waldinger_what_makes_a_good_life_lessons_from_the_longest_study_on_happiness

[3] Waldinger, R. (November, 2015). What Makes a Good Life? Lessons from the Longest study on Happiness [Video File]. Retrieved from https://www.ted.com/talks/robert_waldinger_what_makes_a_good_life_lessons_from_the_longest_study_on_happiness

[4] Smith, Tom W, Peter Marsden, Michael Hout, and Jibum Kim. *General Social Surveys, 1972-2014* [machine-readable data file] /Principal Investigator, Tom W. Smith; Co-Principal Investigator, Peter V. Marsden; Co-Principal Investigator, Michael Hout; Sponsored by National Science Foundation. --NORC ed.-- Chicago: NORC at the University of Chicago [producer]; Storrs, CT: The Roper Center for Public Opinion Research, University of Connecticut [distributor], 2015.

[5] Smith, Tom W, Peter Marsden, Michael Hout, and Jibum Kim. *General Social Surveys, 1972-2014* [machine-readable data file] /Principal Investigator, Tom W. Smith; Co-Principal Investigator, Peter V. Marsden; Co-Principal Investigator, Michael Hout; Sponsored by National Science Foundation. --NORC ed.-- Chicago: NORC at the University of Chicago [producer]; Storrs, CT: The Roper Center for Public Opinion Research,

[6] Wilkinson, K. (2016, September 21) We Are the Generation that Doesn't want Relationships. Retrieved from http://www.huffingtonpost.com/entry/we-are-the-generation-who-doesnt-want-reltionships_us_572131a5e4b03b93e7e435d8

[7] Wiest,B. (2015, May 7) 12 Reasons That Meaningful Relationships are Becoming More and More Rare Retrieved from https://thoughtcatalog.com/brianna-wiest/2015/05/12-reasons-meaningful-relationships-are-becoming-more-and-more-rare/

[8] Braiker, H., & Kelley, H. H. (1979). Conflict in the development of close relationships. In R. L. Burgress, & T. L. Huston (Eds.), Social exchange in developing relationships (pp. 135–168). New York, NY: Academic Press.

CHAPTER 9

[1] Gottfried, P. E. (2001). *After liberalism: mass democracy in the managerial state*. Princeton, NJ. Princeton University Press.

[2] Haidt, J. (2016, November) Can A Divided America Heal [Video File] Retrieved from https://www.ted.com/talks/jonathan_haidt_can_a_divided_america_heal

[3] Haidt, J. (2012). *The righteous mind: Why good people are divided by politics and religion*. New York, NY. Vintage.

CHAPTER 10

[1] Collins, J. (2007). Level 5 leadership. *The Jossey-Bass reader on educational leadership*, *2*, 27-50.

[2] Sunstein, C. R. (2005). *Why societies need dissent* (Vol. 9). Cambridge, MA: Harvard University Press.

[3] Pope, A., & Warburton, W. (1719). *An essay on criticism* (Vol. 11, pp. 84-87). Bernard Lintot.

Wes Parham MBA Ph.D.

Wes Parham MBA Ph.D. is a higher education professional and Director of Training at WEEW Consulting. He is a national speaker in the areas of student development, organizational innovation, and organizational leadership. With his unique mix of social commentary, humor, and scholarship Wes has presented to thousands of students, professionals, and individuals and has established himself as a dynamic voice in today's culture.

Wes earned a Bachelor's degree in communication and an MBA with an emphasis in Leadership and Organizational change from the University of Missouri-Kansas City. He earned his Ph.D. in Organizational Leadership from Regent University in Virginia Beach. He has a true passion for individual empowerment, personal growth, and creative leadership. His professional experiences include positions as a project manager, student life coach, academic advisor, recruiter, scholarship coordinator, consultant, admissions director and more. His newest area of emphasis is on the intersection of selective exposure theory, millennials, and haters. Wes hopes to challenge, grow, and entertain the next generation of students, professionals, and leaders.

For more information or to book Dr. Parham:

dr.w.c.parham@gmail.com
facebook/hatermindset.
www.drwesparham.com

Made in the USA
Lexington, KY
26 May 2018